BOB DYLAN THE LYRICS 1961—2020

THE TIMES
THEY ARE A-CHANGIN'

时代正在改变

鲍勃·迪伦诗歌集 1961—2020
VOL.02

[美] 鲍勃·迪伦 著　李皖 译

中信出版集团 | 北京

时代正在改变
THE TIMES THEY ARE A-CHANGIN'

鲍勃·迪伦的另一面
ANOTHER SIDE OF BOB DYLAN

THE TIMES THEY ARE A-CHANGIN'
时代正在改变

附加歌词 ————————————————————

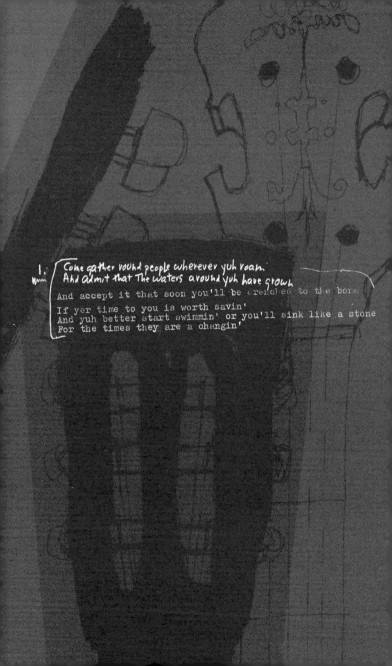

1.

Come gather round people wherever yuh roam
And admit that The waters around yuh have grown

And accept it that soon you'll be drenched to the bone

If yer time to you is worth savin'
And yuh better start swimmin' or you'll sink like a stone
For the times they are a changin'

《时代正在改变》是迪伦的第 3 张录音室专辑，于 1964 年 1 月 13 日由哥伦比亚唱片公司发行。

10 首歌曲全部是迪伦的原创作品，并呈现出一种整体性，这使一张专辑能够成为容纳艺术家完整思想的作品。此后，迪伦的所有专辑几乎都体现了这个特性，并变得越来越鲜明。

专辑的一部分，是主旨鲜明的时代歌曲，涉及社会变革、家乡巨变、价值观撕裂以及对美国官方历史和战争正义性的质疑（《时代正在改变》《北国蓝调》《无休止的告别》《大船入港之际》《上帝在我们这边儿》）。这部分歌曲，最令人惊讶之处是迪伦写出眼前事实的敏锐、揭露历史真相的勇气和告别旧时代的果敢。时间过得越久，他走在时代前面的超前性和洞察力便显得越突出。比如，《北国蓝调》对迅速暴发又迅速没落的北方矿产小镇的书写，不仅与布鲁斯·斯普林斯汀（Bruce Springsteen）笔下 80 年代的美国强烈共振，也让世纪之交大洋彼岸的亚洲人心领神会。

专辑的另一部分，取材于真实的社会事件，大都涉及凶杀，反映种族主义、贫困和公民权等问题。《只是他们棋局里的一颗卒子》书写全美有色人种促进会领袖梅德加·埃弗斯在家门口被暗杀事件，但迪伦并不将凶手指向暗杀者，而是指向他背后的种族隔离势力。《哈蒂·卡罗尔寂寞的死》书写黑人女侍者在餐厅被白人食客用手杖击杀的事件，但是其谴责并不仅仅停留在凶手个人身上，而是指向了整个社会法律及道德的虚伪。《霍利斯·布朗叙事曲》中，布朗因贫穷杀死妻子和 5 个孩子然后自杀的事件似乎骇人听闻，通篇有一种轻描淡写，却恰恰写出了此事最深刻的冷漠和残酷。

还有一部分是情歌。不同于大众普通情歌，这些情歌不仅呈现出迪伦与苏西恋爱后期的复杂心理，也成为具有时代性的向旧事、旧情、旧景毅然作别的个人宣言（《太多这样的早晨》《西班牙皮靴》）。

专辑的标题曲《时代正在改变》，成为迪伦最著名的歌曲之一，许多人认为它抓住了 20 世纪 60 年代社会精神和政治风貌的精髓。不仅如此，在整个 20 世纪历史上，它都展现出一种持久的启发性：世界各地的政治经济变革，使其外延不断延展，并激发出一系列受其影响、具有相近内涵、呈现为不同语言的音乐作品。

该专辑于 1963 年 8 月 6 日开工，断断续续录了 6 场，一直持续到该年 10 月 31 日才收工，从中产生了 10 首专辑收录歌曲，以及 14 首最终被弃用之作。

歌词上，迪伦继续从《圣经》、民歌、法国象征主义、"垮掉的一代"作家以及布莱希特的作品中获得灵感；音乐上，则继续受到凯尔特民歌、苏格兰民歌和英语传统民歌的深刻影响。虽然编曲仍然只有迪伦的木吉他和口琴，但与之前专辑不同，黑人制作人汤姆·威尔逊（Tom Wilson）

的全程制作，给这张专辑带来了更加尖锐、强烈、新颖而丰富的音响风格。威尔逊本是一位爵士乐制作人，对民谣有些看不上，但迪伦的歌词，以及这位年轻白人的黑人布鲁斯式的演唱，让他大为惊异和震动。

在专辑方向上，迪伦的目标感和现实关怀变得更加明确，他全程收敛了嬉皮笑脸，变得分外严肃。这使这张专辑充满了黑色和悲观的情绪，并有一种道德主义的峻急面目。由此引起之前一些歌迷和评论家的不满，认为它缺乏幽默感、自由精神和音乐多样性。

在解读歌曲《时代正在改变》时，迪伦回忆说，创作这首歌时费尽心思，就是要为当下创作一首变革之歌。"这绝对是一首有目的的歌曲。……我想写一首大歌，短而简洁的诗句以催眠的方式相互堆积。民权运动与民歌（复兴）运动一度非常亲近，并在当时结为一体。"

专辑录制完近一个月后，即 1963 年 11 月 22 日，肯尼迪总统在达拉斯遇刺身亡。据友人回忆，听闻消息的那一刻，迪伦说："这意味着他们要告诉你，'别希望改变什么'。"

肯尼迪遇刺 3 周后，美国国家紧急事件公民特权委员会（NECLC）授予迪伦年度汤姆·潘恩公民权利奖，以表彰他对民权运动的贡献。

THE TIMES THEY ARE A-CHANGIN'

Come gather 'round people

Wherever you roam

And admit that the waters

Around you have grown

And accept it that soon

You'll be drenched to the bone

If your time to you is worth savin'

Then you better start swimmin' or you'll sink like a stone

For the times they are a-changin'

Come writers and critics

Who prophesize with your pen

And keep your eyes wide

The chance won't come again

And don't speak too soon

For the wheel's still in spin

And there's no tellin' who that it's namin'

For the loser now will be later to win

For the times they are a-changin'

时代正在改变 [1]

人们啊，来吧，来聚在一起
不管你漂在哪儿，承认吧
那围困你的水
它又往上涨啦
过不多久还得接受
你会湿透，一直到骨头
假如你的时间还值得省
最好开始游，免得沉底儿像块石头
因为时代正在改变

来吧，作家和批评家
用笔写出你们的预言
眼睛要一直张大
机会它不会再来啦
但也不要说得太早
因为轮子还没停下
无法预知谁会被选中
因为现在的输家，日后会变成赢家
因为时代正在改变

---

[1] 本篇由郝佳校译。

Come senators, congressmen
Please heed the call
Don't stand in the doorway
Don't block up the hall
For he that gets hurt
Will be he who has stalled
There's a battle outside and it is ragin'
It'll soon shake your windows and rattle your walls
For the times they are a-changin'

Come mothers and fathers
Throughout the land
And don't criticize
What you can't understand
Your sons and your daughters
Are beyond your command
Your old road is rapidly agin'
Please get out of the new one if you can't lend your hand
For the times they are a-changin'

The line it is drawn
The curse it is cast
The slow one now
Will later be fast
As the present now
Will later be past

来吧，参议员和众议员

请注意这个吁请

不要站在门口

不要堵住走廊

因为那挡路的

接下来就会受伤

外面有场战斗，打得异常凶猛

马上会来摇你的窗，使你的墙嘎嘎响

因为时代正在改变

来吧，母亲和父亲

全国各地的母亲和父亲

不要去批评

你们不理解的事情

你们的儿女

不会听你们的命令

你们的老路子，转眼已不灵

如果不能伸手相助，就请离开这条新路

因为时代正在改变

界线已经划好

咒语已经种下

现在走慢的

以后会快

就像现在这一刻

过会儿即不在

The order is rapidly fadin'

And the first one now will later be last

For the times they are a-changin'

秩序正快速消失
眼下的头名，来日将成最后
因为时代正在改变

BALLAD OF HOLLIS BROWN

Hollis Brown
He lived on the outside of town
Hollis Brown
He lived on the outside of town
With his wife and five children
And his cabin fallin' down

You looked for work and money
And you walked a rugged mile
You looked for work and money
And you walked a rugged mile
Your children are so hungry
That they don't know how to smile

Your baby's eyes look crazy
They're a-tuggin' at your sleeve
Your baby's eyes look crazy
They're a-tuggin' at your sleeve
You walk the floor and wonder why
With every breath you breathe

The rats have got your flour

霍利斯·布朗叙事曲

霍利斯·布朗
住在城外
霍利斯·布朗
住在城外
有老婆和五个孩子
还有快倒塌的房子

要找工作和赚钱
你走了一英里不平路
要找工作和赚钱
你走了一英里不平路
你的孩子饿坏了
早不知笑为何物

你宝贝的眼看着像是疯了
它们在拽你的袖子
你宝贝的眼看着像是疯了
它们在拽你的袖子
你踱来踱去想来由
一口一口喘着气

老鼠吃了你家面粉

Bad blood it got your mare
The rats have got your flour
Bad blood it got your mare
If there's anyone that knows
Is there anyone that cares?

You prayed to the Lord above
Oh please send you a friend
You prayed to the Lord above
Oh please send you a friend
Your empty pockets tell yuh
That you ain't a-got no friend

Your babies are crying louder
It's pounding on your brain
Your babies are crying louder now
It's pounding on your brain
Your wife's screams are stabbin' you
Like the dirty drivin' rain

Your grass it is turning black
There's no water in your well
Your grass is turning black
There's no water in your well
You spent your last lone dollar
On seven shotgun shells

噩运找上你家母马
老鼠吃了你家面粉
噩运找上你家母马
就算有人知道
又有谁会在乎？

你向上祈求恩主
啊，请赐给你朋友
你向上祈求恩主
啊，请赐给你朋友
你空空的衣袋告诉你
你不会有朋友

你的宝贝们越哭越大声
哭声撞着你的头
现在你的宝贝们越哭越大声
哭声撞着你的头
妻子的尖叫在扎你
如同这污浊骤雨

你的草场变黑了
你的井变得干涸
你的草场变黑了
你的井变得干涸
花掉最后一块钱
你买了七颗子弹

Way out in the wilderness
A cold coyote calls
Way out in the wilderness
A cold coyote calls
Your eyes fix on the shotgun
That's hangin' on the wall

Your brain is a-bleedin'
And your legs can't seem to stand
Your brain is a-bleedin'
And your legs can't seem to stand
Your eyes fix on the shotgun
That you're holdin' in your hand

There's seven breezes a-blowin'
All around the cabin door
There's seven breezes a-blowin'
All around the cabin door
Seven shots ring out
Like the ocean's pounding roar

There's seven people dead
On a South Dakota farm
There's seven people dead
On a South Dakota farm

在荒野深处
一头草原狼叫着
在荒野深处
一头草原狼叫着
你两眼盯着猎枪
它就挂在墙上

血往头上冲
双腿好像站不住
血往头上冲
双腿好像站不住
你两眼盯着猎枪
它就握在手上

有七股微风吹
围着那木屋门
有七股微风吹
围着那木屋门
七声枪响呼啸
如同大海轰鸣

有七人死亡
在南达科他农场
有七人死亡
在南达科他农场

Somewhere in the distance

There's seven new people born

遥远的某个地方
有七个新人来到世上

WITH GOD ON OUR SIDE

Oh my name it is nothin'
My age it means less
The country I come from
Is called the Midwest
I's taught and brought up there
The laws to abide
And that the land that I live in
Has God on its side

Oh the history books tell it
They tell it so well
The cavalries charged
The Indians fell
The cavalries charged
The Indians died
Oh the country was young
With God on its side

Oh the Spanish-American
War had its day
And the Civil War too
Was soon laid away

上帝在我们这边儿

噢，我的名字啥都不是
我的年龄也毫无意义
我来自的地区
人们管它叫中西部
我在那儿受了教育
他们叫我从小遵守法律
我生活的这片地方
上帝在它的一边儿

噢，历史书是这么说的
上面写得很清楚
骑兵队向前冲
印第安人倒下了
骑兵队向前冲
印第安人完了
噢，这国家很年轻
上帝在它的这边儿

噢，美西战争
激战一时
而内战
也很快过去

And the names of the heroes
I's made to memorize
With guns in their hands
And God on their side

Oh the First World War, boys
It closed out its fate
The reason for fighting
I never got straight
But I learned to accept it
Accept it with pride
For you don't count the dead
When God's on your side

When the Second World War
Came to an end
We forgave the Germans
And we were friends
Though they murdered six million
In the ovens they fried
The Germans now too
Have God on their side

I've learned to hate Russians
All through my whole life
If another war starts

英雄们的名字
他们要我记住
他们手里有枪
上帝在他们那边儿

噢，第一次世界大战，天哪
竟气数到头打完了
那打仗的原因
我一直没弄清楚
但是我学会了接受它
怀着自豪接受
你不会数死者的数目
当上帝在你那边儿

第二次世界大战
结束了
我们原谅了德国人
而且我们是朋友
尽管他们杀了六百万人
用他们制造的焚化炉
德国人现在
把上帝也弄到了他们一边儿

我学会了恨俄国人
这恨将贯穿我的一生
如果又一场大战打响

It's them we must fight

To hate them and fear them

To run and to hide

And accept it all bravely

With God on my side

But now we got weapons

Of the chemical dust

If fire them we're forced to

Then fire them we must

One push of the button

And a shot the world wide

And you never ask questions

When God's on your side

Through many dark hour

I've been thinkin' about this

That Jesus Christ

Was betrayed by a kiss

But I can't think for you

You'll have to decide

Whether Judas Iscariot

Had God on his side

So now as I'm leavin'

I'm weary as Hell

他们就是我们的敌人
恨他们，怕他们
逃跑，或躲起来
然而还是要勇敢地接受
上帝在我这边儿

而现在我们有了
化学尘埃的武器
既然要跟他们打
那就必须跟他们打
按一下那按钮
一个全球性打击
而你从不会提问
当上帝在你这边儿

很多黑暗的时刻
我一直这么想着
想着耶稣基督
是被一个吻出卖的
但我不能代你思考
这必须由你作出判定
是否加略人犹大
让上帝站到了他那边儿

所以现在我要走了
我累得要死了

The confusion I'm feelin'

Ain't no tongue can tell

The words fill my head

And fall to the floor

If God's on our side

He'll stop the next war

心里乱极了
没办法说清楚
言语塞满了我脑海
然后掉落到了地上
如果上帝在我们这边儿
他应该阻止下一场大战

ONE TOO MANY MORNINGS

Down the street the dogs are barkin'
And the day is a-gettin' dark
As the night comes in a-fallin'
The dogs'll lose their bark
An' the silent night will shatter
From the sounds inside my mind
For I'm one too many mornings
And a thousand miles behind

From the crossroads of my doorstep
My eyes they start to fade
As I turn my head back to the room
Where my love and I have laid
An' I gaze back to the street
The sidewalk and the sign
And I'm one too many mornings
An' a thousand miles behind

It's a restless hungry feeling
That don't mean no one no good

太多这样的早晨 [1]

狗在街上叫着

天快要黑了

当夜幕垂落

狗吠声将止歇

而静夜将被我

内心的声音击碎

因为我已被太多这样的早晨

被迢迢一千英里，丢在了后面

从我家门前的十字路

我的视线开始黯淡

当我回转头

看着我的爱和我同眠的房间

然后我回眸凝视街道

那人行道和路标

而我已被太多这样的早晨

被迢迢一千英里，丢在了后面

那是无休止的饥饿感

对每个人都不妙

---

[1]　本篇由杨盈盈校译。

When ev'rything I'm a-sayin'

You can say it just as good

You're right from your side

I'm right from mine

We're both just one too many mornings

An' a thousand miles behind

我要说的每句话
你都能说得一样好
在你看来你是对的
在我看来我都正确
我们俩都已被太多这样的早晨
被迢迢一千英里，丢在了后面

NORTH COUNTRY BLUES

Come gather 'round friends
And I'll tell you a tale
Of when the red iron pits ran plenty
But the cardboard filled windows
And old men on the benches
Tell you now that the whole town is empty

In the north end of town
My own children are grown
But I was raised on the other
In the wee hours of youth
My mother took sick
And I was brought up by my brother

The iron ore poured
As the years passed the door
The drag lines an' the shovels they was a-humming
'Til one day my brother
Failed to come home
The same as my father before him

Well a long winter's wait

北国蓝调

朋友们请聚拢来
我给大家讲个故事
关于红铁矿蓬蓬勃勃
但硬纸板塞满了窗户的年代
而长椅上的老人
告诉你全镇如今已经空了

在镇子最北面
我的孩子们出生长大
而我成长于另一端
在我刚记事时
我的母亲病了
我是哥哥带大的

铁矿石倾泻
随岁月从门前流过
挖掘机车队和铲车轰鸣
直到一天我哥哥
没能回家
一如他之前我的父亲

噢，一个长冬的煎熬

From the window I watched

My friends they couldn't have been kinder

And my schooling was cut

As I quit in the spring

To marry John Thomas, a miner

Oh the years passed again

And the givin' was good

With the lunch bucket filled every season

What with three babies born

The work was cut down

To a half a day's shift with no reason

Then the shaft was soon shut

And more work was cut

And the fire in the air, it felt frozen

'Til a man come to speak

And he said in one week

That number eleven was closin'

They complained in the East

They are paying too high

They say that your ore ain't worth digging

That it's much cheaper down

In the South American towns

Where the miners work almost for nothing

我在窗口张望
伙伴们待我不能再好
但我的学业还是戛然而止
我在春天辍学
嫁给了约翰·托马斯，一名矿工

啊，岁月再度奔流
而且赏赐丰厚
四季的午餐桶桶溢满
随着三个孩子出世
工作被缩减成半天
没有缘由

不久后矿井关了
更多的工作被砍掉
空中的火，像是冻住了
直到一个人过来告知
说再过一星期
十一号井将关闭

东部的人抱怨
他们支出太高
说你们的矿不值得采
在南美洲的镇子里
矿石便宜得多
那儿的矿工几乎不要钱

So the mining gates locked
And the red iron rotted
And the room smelled heavy from drinking
Where the sad, silent song
Made the hour twice as long
As I waited for the sun to go sinking

I lived by the window
As he talked to himself
This silence of tongues it was building
Then one morning's wake
The bed it was bare
And I's left alone with three children

The summer is gone
The ground's turning cold
The stores one by one they're a-foldin'
My children will go
As soon as they grow
Well, there ain't nothing here now to hold them

因此矿区大门锁了
任由红铁矿烂掉
而屋子里都是浓浓酒气
伤心的、沉静的歌声
使时光加倍漫长
当我守着夕阳西沉

我靠着窗边度日
而他喃喃自语
无言的沉默堆积
直到一天早晨醒来
床空了
我被丢下了，一个人带着三个孩子

夏天过去
大地转冷
商店一家家倒闭
我的孩子一旦长大
也会离去
唉，这里再没什么能留住他们

ONLY A PAWN IN THEIR GAME

A bullet from the back of a bush took Medgar Evers' blood
A finger fired the trigger to his name
A handle hid out in the dark
A hand set the spark
Two eyes took the aim
Behind a man's brain
But he can't be blamed
He's only a pawn in their game

A South politician preaches to the poor white man
"You got more than the blacks, don't complain
You're better than them, you been born with white skin,"
    they explain
And the Negro's name
Is used it is plain
For the politician's gain
As he rises to fame
And the poor white remains
On the caboose of the train

只是他们棋局里的一颗卒子

一株灌木后的枪弹取了梅德加·埃弗斯[1] 的血
一根指头朝他的名字扣下了扳机
一个枪柄藏在黑暗里
一只手触发了火
两只眼瞄准了
一个男人的后脑
但不能归罪于他
他只是他们棋局里的一颗卒子

一个南方政客劝诫那个穷苦白人
"你拿的比黑人多,别抱怨了
你比他们强,生来就是白皮肤",
　诸如此类
滥用着"黑鬼"的名字
获取政客的利益
这再明白不过
就在他名声大噪之际
那穷苦白人依旧
坐在火车尾部

---

[1] 梅德加·埃弗斯(1925—1963),美国非裔民权人士。1963 年 6 月
　　12 日在家门前下车时遇刺身亡。

But it ain't him to blame

He's only a pawn in their game

The deputy sheriffs, the soldiers, the governors get paid

And the marshals and cops get the same

But the poor white man's used in the hands of them all like a
  tool

He's taught in his school

From the start by the rule

That the laws are with him

To protect his white skin

To keep up his hate

So he never thinks straight

'Bout the shape that he's in

But it ain't him to blame

He's only a pawn in their game

From the poverty shacks, he looks from the cracks to the tracks

And the hoofbeats pound in his brain

And he's taught how to walk in a pack

Shoot in the back

With his fist in a clinch

To hang and to lynch

To hide 'neath the hood

To kill with no pain

Like a dog on a chain

但这不能归罪于他

他只是他们棋局里的一颗卒子

县警、士兵、州长都有工资

法警和城警也一样

而那个穷苦白人像个工具被玩弄于

　　股掌

从学校上学开始

他就被教会了这一条

法律与他同在

会保护他的白皮肤

会保持他的仇恨

所以他从不去思考

自己的处境

但这不能归罪于他

他只是他们棋局里的一颗卒子

他出身于棚户，从裂缝里望着铁轨

蹄声在脑中嗒嗒作响

他还被教会了如何拉帮结派

从背后开枪

握紧拳头

把人吊死，给人上私刑

脸藏在兜帽下

毫无痛苦地杀人

像链子拴的一条狗

He ain't got no name

But it ain't him to blame

He's only a pawn in their game

Today, Medgar Evers was buried from the bullet he caught

They lowered him down as a king

But when the shadowy sun sets on the one

That fired the gun

He'll see by his grave

On the stone that remains

Carved next to his name

His epitaph plain:

Only a pawn in their game

无名无姓
但这不能归罪于他
他只是他们棋局里的一颗卒子

今天，梅德加·埃弗斯因中弹而下葬
他被缓缓放入墓穴就像国王
而当幽暗的阳光落在
开枪那人的身上
他会看到自己的墓地
那留下的石碑
紧挨着他的名字
那墓志铭刻得简单明白：
只是他们棋局里的一颗卒子

BOOTS OF SPANISH LEATHER

Oh, I'm sailin' away my own true love
I'm sailin' away in the morning
Is there something I can send you from across the sea
From the place that I'll be landing?

No, there's nothin' you can send me, my own true love
There's nothin' I wish to be ownin'
Just carry yourself back to me unspoiled
From across that lonesome ocean

Oh, but I just thought you might want something fine
Made of silver or of golden
Either from the mountains of Madrid
Or from the coast of Barcelona

Oh, but if I had the stars from the darkest night
And the diamonds from the deepest ocean
I'd forsake them all for your sweet kiss
For that's all I'm wishin' to be ownin'

西班牙皮靴

啊，我就要远航了我的挚爱
明早我就要远航
从大洋彼岸我能寄给你什么呢
从我要靠岸的地方？

不，没什么需要寄给我，我的挚爱
我什么东西都不奢望
只要你好好回到我身旁
越过那寂寥孤独的海洋

啊，可我觉得你需要一样宝物
白银或者黄金制成
要么来自马德里山岭
要么来自巴塞罗那海滨

啊，纵使我有最黑暗夜晚的星辰
加上最深海洋中的钻石
我也都会舍弃，只求你甜蜜一吻
那才是我唯一想要的

---

[1]　本篇由杨盈盈校译。

That I might be gone a long time
And it's only that I'm askin'
Is there something I can send you to remember me by
To make your time more easy passin'

Oh, how can, how can you ask me again
It only brings me sorrow
The same thing I want from you today
I would want again tomorrow

I got a letter on a lonesome day
It was from her ship a-sailin'
Saying I don't know when I'll be comin' back again
It depends on how I'm a-feelin'

Well, if you, my love, must think that-a-way
I'm sure your mind is roamin'
I'm sure your heart is not with me
But with the country to where you're goin'

So take heed, take heed of the western wind
Take heed of the stormy weather
And yes, there's something you can send back to me
Spanish boots of Spanish leather

然而可能我会离开很久
所以我只是想问
寄给你什么会让你记起我
让你的时间更易度过

啊，你怎能、怎能还这样问
这只会让我伤悲
今天我向你要的这一样
明天我还想再要一回

寂寞的日子我收到一封信
是从她的船上寄来的
信上说"我不知何日归程
一切取决于我的感觉"

好吧，我的爱，如果你，非这么想
我肯定你的心正在游离
肯定你的心不在我这里
而在你正前往的国度

所以要小心啊，小心那西风
小心那暴风雨天气
哦对了，有样东西你可以寄给我
西班牙皮革制的西班牙靴子

WHEN THE SHIP COMES IN

Oh the time will come up
When the winds will stop
And the breeze will cease to be breathin'
Like the stillness in the wind
'Fore the hurricane begins
The hour when the ship comes in

Oh the seas will split
And the ship will hit
And the sands on the shoreline will be shaking
Then the tide will sound
And the wind will pound
And the morning will be breaking

Oh the fishes will laugh
As they swim out of the path
And the seagulls they'll be smiling
And the rocks on the sand
Will proudly stand
The hour that the ship comes in

And the words that are used

大船入港之际

啊，这时刻终将来临
大风不再吹
微风屏住呼吸
就像风中的静止
在飓风开始之前
在大船入港之际

啊，大海会分开
而大船会到来
海岸线上的沙会震动
然后潮汐轰鸣
而后大风呼啸
而后清晨破晓而生

啊，鱼群会大笑
一边游出航道
而海鸥将微笑
沙滩上的石头
将骄傲地挺立
在大船入港之际

而人们所用的语言

For to get the ship confused

Will not be understood as they're spoken

For the chains of the sea

Will have busted in the night

And will be buried at the bottom of the ocean

A song will lift

As the mainsail shifts

And the boat drifts on to the shoreline

And the sun will respect

Every face on the deck

The hour that the ship comes in

Then the sands will roll

Out a carpet of gold

For your weary toes to be a-touchin'

And the ship's wise men

Will remind you once again

That the whole wide world is watchin'

Oh the foes will rise

With the sleep still in their eyes

And they'll jerk from their beds and think they're dreamin'

But they'll pinch themselves and squeal

And know that it's for real

The hour when the ship comes in

徒增大船困扰
说出来也不被理解
因为大海的锁链
将在夜里崩碎
并埋葬进洋底

一首歌将升起
当主帆变换方向
而小船将向海岸线漂去
太阳会向甲板上每张脸
恭敬致意
在大船入港之际

然后沙滩会展开
一张黄金地毯
让你疲惫的脚趾轻触
而大船上的智者们
将再一次提醒你
整个世界都在关注

啊，敌人们会爬起来
眼睛里还带着睡意
他们从床上跳起来以为是在做梦
但他们会掐自己，尖叫
明白这都是真的
在大船入港之际

Then they'll raise their hands

Sayin' we'll meet all your demands

But we'll shout from the bow your days are numbered

And like Pharoah's tribe

They'll be drownded in the tide

And like Goliath, they'll be conquered

然后他们高举双手
说我们将满足你们的一切要求
但我们从那船头喊，你们的日子到头了
就像法老的部落
他们将被潮水淹没
就像歌利亚，他们将被征服

THE LONESOME DEATH OF HATTIE CARROLL

William Zanzinger killed poor Hattie Carroll
With a cane that he twirled around his diamond ring finger
At a Baltimore hotel society gath'rin'
And the cops were called in and his weapon took from him
As they rode him in custody down to the station
And booked William Zanzinger for first-degree murder
But you who philosophize disgrace and criticize all fears
Take the rag away from your face
Now ain't the time for your tears

William Zanzinger, who at twenty-four years
Owns a tobacco farm of six hundred acres
With rich wealthy parents who provide and protect him
And high office relations in the politics of Maryland
Reacted to his deed with a shrug of his shoulders
And swear words and sneering, and his tongue it was snarling
In a matter of minutes on bail was out walking

哈蒂·卡罗尔寂寞的死 [1]

威廉·赞津格杀害了可怜的哈蒂·卡罗尔
用一根绕着他戴钻戒的手指飞转的手杖
在巴尔的摩一家酒店的社团聚会上
警察接报出警，收走了他的武器
将他拘押去警局
并将威廉·赞津格列为一级杀人嫌疑犯
但把耻辱哲学化并批评一切恐惧的你
把帕子从脸上拿开吧
现在还不是流泪的时候

威廉·赞津格，二十四岁
拥有一个六百英亩的烟草农场
和供养与保护他的有钱爹妈
以及马里兰州政界的高层关系
对自己的所作所为，他的回应是耸耸肩
还有脏话和讥讽，他的舌头一直在吠叫
只几分钟就被保释出来

---

[1] 歌曲取材自真实事件——1963 年 2 月 9 日，在巴尔的摩一家酒店
的舞会上，24 岁的白人青年威廉·赞津格嫌 51 岁的黑人女服务员
哈蒂·卡罗尔上酒不够快，辱骂并用手杖打伤了她，卡罗尔于 8 小
时后不治身亡。

But you who philosophize disgrace and criticize all fears

Take the rag away from your face

Now ain't the time for your tears

Hattie Carroll was a maid of the kitchen

She was fifty-one years old and gave birth to ten children

Who carried the dishes and took out the garbage

And never sat once at the head of the table

And didn't even talk to the people at the table

Who just cleaned up all the food from the table

And emptied the ashtrays on a whole other level

Got killed by a blow, lay slain by a cane

That sailed through the air and came down through the room

Doomed and determined to destroy all the gentle

And she never done nothing to William Zanzinger

But you who philosophize disgrace and criticize all fears

Take the rag away from your face

Now ain't the time for your tears

In the courtroom of honor, the judge pounded his gavel

To show that all's equal and that the courts are on the level

And that the strings in the books ain't pulled and persuaded

And that even the nobles get properly handled

Once that the cops have chased after and caught 'em

And that the ladder of law has no top and no bottom

Stared at the person who killed for no reason

但把耻辱哲学化并批评一切恐惧的你
把帕子从脸上拿开吧
现在还不是流泪的时候

哈蒂·卡罗尔是名厨房女佣
五十一岁，生了十个孩子
她端盘子倒垃圾
一次也没上过桌
甚至不曾与桌上的人说话
她只是收拾干净桌上的食物
清空另一层楼的烟灰缸
就被一记重击打死，被一根手杖击杀
手杖飞行空中，穿过房间落下
注定和决意要摧毁这位温良女性
而她从未对威廉·赞津格做过什么
但把耻辱哲学化并批评一切恐惧的你
把帕子从脸上拿开吧
现在还不是流泪的时候

在正义的法庭上，法官重重敲响木槌
以示人人平等，法院公正
而且法律条文不容操纵与游说
就算是贵族也会受到应得的处置
一旦被警察追捕缉拿归案
那么法律的阶梯无顶也无底
盯视着眼前这个人，他杀人无缘无由

Who just happened to be feelin' that way without warnin'

And he spoke through his cloak, most deep and distinguished

And handed out strongly, for penalty and repentance

William Zanzinger with a six-month sentence

Oh, but you who philosophize disgrace and criticize all fears

Bury the rag deep in your face

For now's the time for your tears

只是心血来潮，毫无预兆
法官说话了，透过极度深沉且尊贵的法袍
坚定地做出宣判，为了惩戒并促其忏悔
威廉·赞津格被判处徒刑六个月
哦，但把耻辱哲学化并批评一切恐惧的你
把帕子深埋进脸里吧
因为现在该是流泪的时候了

RESTLESS FAREWELL

Oh all the money that in my whole life I did spend

Be it mine right or wrongfully

I let it slip gladly past the hands of my friends

To tie up the time most forcefully

But the bottles are done

We've killed each one

And the table's full and overflowed

And the corner sign

Says it's closing time

So I'll bid farewell and be down the road

Oh ev'ry girl that ever I've touched

I did not do it harmfully

And ev'ry girl that ever I've hurt

I did not do it knowin'ly

But to remain as friends

And make amends

You need the time and stay behind

And since my feet are now fast

And point away from the past

I'll bid farewell and be down the line

无休止的告别

啊，我这辈子花的钱
不管正当所得还是不义之财
都让它很愉快地流经朋友们的手
最有力地将时间系住
但是瓶子空了
我们把每瓶酒都干掉了
桌子满得溢出来了
而角落的牌子
写着打烊了
所以我要告别，上路

啊，每一位我爱抚过的姑娘
我这么做并非出于恶意
而每一位我伤害过的姑娘
我这么做也并非故意
只是要继续做朋友
并弥补过失
你需要时间留在原处
而由于我步履匆匆
背离过去前行
所以我要告别，上路

Oh ev'ry foe that ever I faced

The cause was there before we came

And ev'ry cause that ever I fought

I fought it full without regret or shame

But the dark does die

As the curtain is drawn and somebody's eyes

Must meet the dawn

And if I see the day

I'd only have to stay

So I'll bid farewell in the night and be gone

Oh, ev'ry thought that's strung a knot in my mind

I might go insane if it couldn't be sprung

But it's not to stand naked under unknowin' eyes

It's for myself and my friends my stories are sung

But the time ain't tall, yet on time you depend

And no word is possessed by no special friend

And though the line is cut

It ain't quite the end

I'll just bid farewell till we meet again

Oh a false clock tries to tick out my time

To disgrace, distract, and bother me

And the dirt of gossip blows into my face

And the dust of rumors covers me

But if the arrow is straight

啊，每一个我遇到的敌手
我们来之前怨愤已定
对每一个我要打击的目标
我全力以赴无愧无悔
但是黑暗终会消逝
当窗帘拉开，一个人的眼睛
必须迎接黎明
如果我看到了白昼
就必然会留下来
所以我会在夜里告别，离去

啊，每一个在我心里打结的想法
如果不将它打开，我可能会发疯
但我不能赤裸地站在无知者面前
我的故事要唱给自己和朋友们听
可是时日不多，你又只能倚仗它
任什么话都不会被哪位贵友单独留下
尽管线索断了
也绝非就是尽头
所以我只是告别，咱们后会有期

啊，一台假时钟想磨碎我的时间
想羞辱我、分裂我、干扰我
而流言的泥扑进了脸
谣言的灰将我遮掩
但如果箭是直的

And the point is slick

It can pierce through dust no matter how thick

So I'll make my stand

And remain as I am

And bid farewell and not give a damn

箭头锋利
再厚的灰它也能洞穿
所以我会坚守立场
保持自己的模样
然后告别，毫不在意

ETERNAL CIRCLE

I sang the song slowly
As she stood in the shadows
She stepped to the light
As my silver strings spun
She called with her eyes
To the tune I's a-playin'
But the song it was long
And I'd only begun

Through a bullet of light
Her face was reflectin'
The fast fading words
That rolled from my tongue
With a long-distance look
Her eyes was on fire
But the song it was long
And there was more to be sung

My eyes danced a circle
Across her clear outline
With her head tilted sideways
She called me again

永恒的循环

我缓缓唱着这首歌
此时她立在阴影里
等她移步灯下
我的银弦转急
她用眼睛呼唤
应和我弹奏的旋律
但这首歌很长
我只是刚开始

透过一束光
她的脸映射着
从我舌尖滚过的
快速黯淡的词句
远远地望过去
她的眼像燃起了火
但这首歌很长
还有更多没唱

我的目光舞成圆
环绕着她清晰的身影
她把头侧向一边
将我再一次呼唤

As the tune drifted out

She breathed hard through the echo

But the song it was long

And it was far to the end

I glanced at my guitar

And played it pretendin'

That of all the eyes out there

I could see none

As her thoughts pounded hard

Like the pierce of an arrow

But the song it was long

And it had to get done

As the tune finally folded

I laid down the guitar

Then looked for the girl

Who'd stayed for so long

But her shadow was missin'

For all of my searchin'

So I picked up my guitar

And began the next song

随着旋律飘出
穿越回声她呼吸急促
但这首歌很长
距唱完还很远

我扫了一眼吉他
继续弹奏
假装台下所有眼睛
我都没看见
当她的思绪猛烈袭来
犹如飞箭洞穿
但这首歌很长
我必须把它唱完

全曲终告完成
我放下吉他
然后寻找那位
待了许久的姑娘
但是寻寻觅觅
不见伊人影踪
于是我拿起吉他
开始下一首歌曲

PATHS OF VICTORY

Trails of troubles
Roads of battles
Paths of victory
I shall walk

The trail is dusty
And my road it might be rough
But the better roads are waiting
And boys it ain't far off

Trails of troubles
Roads of battles
Paths of victory
We shall walk

I walked down by the river
I turned my head up high
I saw that silver linin'
That was hangin' in the sky

胜利之路

纷扰之径
斗争之途
胜利之路
我迈开大步

小径上尘土飞扬
我的路或许坎坷
但是佳境渐入
伙计们，目标在望

纷扰之径
斗争之途
胜利之路
我们迈开大步

沿着江河走
头颅高昂
看见那银线 [1]
挂在天上

---

[1] 银线，指云朵的银色边缘，比喻一线希望。

Trails of troubles
Roads of battles
Paths of victory
We shall walk

The evenin' dusk was rollin'
I was walking down the track
There was a one-way wind a-blowin'
And it was blowin' at my back

Trails of troubles
Roads of battles
Paths of victory
We shall walk

The gravel road is bumpy
It's a hard road to ride
But there's a clearer road a-waitin'
With the cinders on the side

Trails of troubles
Roads of battles
Paths of victory
We shall walk

That evening train was rollin'

纷扰之径
斗争之途
胜利之路
我们迈开大步

暮色在翻滚
我一路沿着铁轨
风一去不回
吹打着我的后背

纷扰之径
斗争之途
胜利之路
我们迈开大步

砾石路崎岖不平
难以驱车驰骋
但光明坦途在望
煤渣扫落两旁

纷扰之径
斗争之途
胜利之路
我们迈开大步

夜行列车摇晃着

The hummin' of its wheels
My eyes they saw a better day
As I looked across the fields

Trails of troubles
Roads of battles
Paths of victory
We shall walk

The trail is dusty
The road it might be rough
But the good road is a-waitin'
And boys it ain't far off

Trails of troubles
Roads of battles
Paths of victory
We shall walk

车轮的嗡嗡哼唱
我看到更美好的日子
当双眼越过远方

纷扰之径
斗争之途
胜利之路
我们迈开大步

小径上尘土飞扬
这条路或许坎坷
但是佳境渐入
伙计们，目标在望

纷扰之径
斗争之途
胜利之路
我们迈开大步

ONLY A HOBO

As I was out walking on a corner one day
I spied an old hobo, in a doorway he lay
His face was all grounded in the cold sidewalk floor
And I guess he'd been there for the whole night or more

Only a hobo, but one more is gone
Leavin' nobody to sing his sad song
Leavin' nobody to carry him home
Only a hobo, but one more is gone

A blanket of newspaper covered his head
As the curb was his pillow, the street was his bed
One look at his face showed the hard road he'd come
And a fistful of coins showed the money he bummed

Only a hobo, but one more is gone
Leavin' nobody to sing his sad song
Leavin' nobody to carry him home
Only a hobo, but one more is gone

Does it take much of a man to see his whole life go down
To look up on the world from a hole in the ground

只是个流浪汉

有一天我出门走过街角
看见一个老流浪汉，躺在门口
他整个脸贴着人行道冰冷的地面
我想他在那儿至少已经有整整一晚

只是个流浪汉，可是又走了一个
身后无人为他唱哀歌
身后无人带他回家
只是个流浪汉，可是又走了一个

一张报纸毯子盖着他的头
马路牙子作枕头，街道是床
看一眼他的脸即知他一路艰难
一拳头的硬币是他讨来的钱

只是个流浪汉，可是又走了一个
身后无人为他唱哀歌
身后无人带他回家
只是个流浪汉，可是又走了一个

一个人看到自己一生没落是否沉痛不已
从地洞里抬头看人世

To wait for your future like a horse that's gone lame
To lie in the gutter and die with no name?

Only a hobo, but one more is gone
Leavin' nobody to sing his sad song
Leavin' nobody to carry him home
Only a hobo, but one more is gone

像一匹瘸马等待未来
躺在排水沟里无名无姓地离开？

只是个流浪汉，可是又走了一个
身后无人为他唱哀歌
身后无人带他回家
只是个流浪汉，可是又走了一个

LAY DOWN YOUR WEARY TUNE

Lay down your weary tune, lay down
Lay down the song you strum
And rest yourself 'neath the strength of strings
No voice can hope to hum

Struck by the sounds before the sun
I knew the night had gone
The morning breeze like a bugle blew
Against the drums of dawn

Lay down your weary tune, lay down
Lay down the song you strum
And rest yourself 'neath the strength of strings
No voice can hope to hum

The ocean wild like an organ played
The seaweed's wove its strands
The crashin' waves like cymbals clashed
Against the rocks and sands

Lay down your weary tune, lay down
Lay down the song you strum

歇下你疲惫的曲调

歇下你疲惫的曲调，歇下吧
歇下你不经心弹奏的歌
让自己歇息在琴弦力量下面
任何声音都不许发出

被日出前的声响敲醒
我知道黑夜已去
晨风如号角劲吹
对阵那黎明的鼓

歇下你疲惫的曲调，歇下吧
歇下你不经心弹奏的歌
让自己歇息在琴弦力量下面
任何声音都不许发出

大海狂野如风琴奏起
它的弦索是海草编织
拍岸的惊涛如同铙钹
冲撞着礁石和沙砾

歇下你疲惫的曲调，歇下吧
歇下你不经心弹奏的歌

And rest yourself 'neath the strength of strings
No voice can hope to hum

I stood unwound beneath the skies
And clouds unbound by laws
The cryin' rain like a trumpet sang
And asked for no applause

Lay down your weary tune, lay down
Lay down the song you strum
And rest yourself 'neath the strength of strings
No voice can hope to hum

The last of leaves fell from the trees
And clung to a new love's breast
The branches bare like a banjo played
To the winds that listened best

I gazed down in the river's mirror
And watched its winding strum
The water smooth ran like a hymn
And like a harp did hum

Lay down your weary tune, lay down
Lay down the song you strum
And rest yourself 'neath the strength of strings
No voice can hope to hum

让自己歇息在琴弦力量下面
任何声音都不许发出

我无牵无绊伫立天空下
云朵也不拘于任何法律
哭泣的雨像小号在歌唱
并不期求有谁鼓掌欢呼

歇下你疲惫的曲调，歇下吧
歇下你不经心弹奏的歌
让自己歇息在琴弦力量下面
任何声音都不许发出

最后的树叶从林中飘落
偎依在新恋人的怀中
新裸的树枝像班卓琴奏鸣
给最认真倾听的风

我低头凝视河面之镜
细看它蜿蜒的轻柔拨弄
河水奔流像首赞美诗
又像竖琴发出了低吟

歇下你疲惫的曲调，歇下吧
歇下你不经心弹奏的歌
让自己歇息在琴弦力量下面
任何声音都不许发出

PERCY'S SONG

Bad news, bad news
Come to me where I sleep
Turn, turn, turn again
Sayin' one of your friends
Is in trouble deep
Turn, turn to the rain
And the wind

Tell me the trouble
Tell once to my ear
Turn, turn, turn again
Joliet prison
And ninety-nine years
Turn, turn to the rain
And the wind

Oh what's the charge
Of how this came to be
Turn, turn, turn again
Manslaughter

珀西之歌 [1]

坏消息，坏消息
传到了我睡下的地方
转，转，再转
说是你一个朋友
深陷困境
转，转向雨
转向风

讲讲是何困境
对着我耳朵说一遍
转，转，再转
乔利埃特监狱
并且九十九年
转，转向雨
转向风

啊，指控什么
导致如此结果
转，转，再转
过失杀人

---

[1] 本篇由杨盈盈校译。

In the highest of degree
Turn, turn to the rain
And the wind

I sat down and wrote
The best words I could write
Turn, turn, turn again
Explaining to the judge
I'd be there on Wednesday night
Turn, turn to the rain
And the wind

Without a reply
I left by the moon
Turn, turn, turn again
And was in his chambers
By the next afternoon
Turn, turn to the rain
And the wind

Could ya tell me the facts?
I said without fear
Turn, turn, turn again
That a friend of mine
Would get ninety-nine years
Turn, turn to the rain

顶级重罪
转，转向雨
转向风

我坐下来写
尽力写出最好的文字
转，转，再转
向法官言明
我周三晚上到
转，转向雨
转向风

没有回音
我借月色出门
转，转，再转
次日午后
进了他办公室
转，转向雨
转向风

你可否告我实情？
我问，全无惧色
转，转，再转
那是我一个朋友
被判了九十九年
转，转向雨

And the wind

A crash on the highway
Flew the car to a field
Turn, turn, turn again
There was four persons killed
And he was at the wheel
Turn, turn to the rain
And the wind

But I knew him as good
As I'm knowin' myself
Turn, turn, turn again
And he wouldn't harm a life
That belonged to someone else
Turn, turn to the rain
And the wind

The judge spoke
Out of the side of his mouth
Turn, turn, turn again
Sayin', "The witness who saw
He left little doubt"
Turn, turn to the rain
And the wind

转向风

是公路车祸
车子飞进农田
转，转，再转
四人死亡
车是他开的
转，转向雨
转向风

但我很了解他
就像了解我自己
转，转，再转
他不会伤害
他人性命
转，转向雨
转向风

法官说话了
从嘴巴一角
转，转，再转
说："有目击证人
案子几无疑问"
转，转向雨
转向风

That may be true

He's got a sentence to serve

Turn, turn, turn again

But ninety-nine years

He just don't deserve

Turn, turn to the rain

And the wind

Too late, too late

For his case it is sealed

Turn, turn, turn again

His sentence is passed

And it cannot be repealed

Turn, turn to the rain

And the wind

But he ain't no criminal

And his crime it is none

Turn, turn, turn again

What happened to him

Could happen to anyone

Turn, turn to the rain

And the wind

And at that the judge jerked forward

And his face it did freeze

这或许属实
他已获罪要去服刑
转，转，再转
但九十九年
不是他应得的
转，转向雨
转向风

晚了，晚了
他的案子已结
转，转，再转
判决已经宣布
不能撤销
转，转向雨
转向风

但他不是罪犯
他并没有犯罪
转，转，再转
他所发生的
任何人都可能遇上
转，转向雨
转向风

听到这话，法官向前一探
他的脸确实僵住啦

Turn, turn, turn again

Sayin', "Could you kindly leave

My office now, please"

Turn, turn to the rain

And the wind

Well his eyes looked funny

And I stood up so slow

Turn, turn, turn again

With no other choice

Except for to go

Turn, turn to the rain

And the wind

I walked down the hallway

And I heard his door slam

Turn, turn, turn again

I walked down the courthouse stairs

And I did not understand

Turn, turn to the rain

And the wind

And I played my guitar

Through the night to the day

Turn, turn, turn again

And the only tune

转，转，再转
他说："可否请您，立即
离开我的办公室"
转，转向雨
转向风

哦他的眼神滑稽
而我缓缓起身
转，转，再转
除了走人
别无选择
转，转向雨
转向风

我走向门廊
听见门砰地关上
转，转，再转
我走下法院楼梯
我无法理解
转，转向雨
转向风

于是我弹吉他
从夜晚弹到天明
转，转，再转
而我的吉他弹出的

My guitar could play

Was, "Oh the Cruel Rain

And the Wind"

唯一的曲调是：
"啊无情的雨
无情的风"

GUESS I'M DOIN' FINE

Well, I ain't got my childhood
Or friends I once did know
No, I ain't got my childhood
Or friends I once did know
But I still got my voice left
I can take it anywhere I go
Hey, hey, so I guess I'm doin' fine

And I've never had much money
But I'm still around somehow
No, I've never had much money
But I'm still around somehow
Many times I've bended
But I ain't never yet bowed
Hey, hey, so I guess I'm doin' fine

Trouble, oh trouble
I've trouble on my mind
Trouble, oh trouble
Trouble on my mind
But the trouble in the world, Lord
Is much more bigger than mine

我想我过得不错

嗯，我没有了童年
也没有了熟悉的朋友
是的，我没有了童年
也没有了熟悉的朋友
但我还有我的嗓音
我可以带着它到处走
嗨，嗨，所以我想我过得不错

我从没有很多钱
但总还能莫名其妙露露脸
是的，我从没有很多钱
但总还能莫名其妙露露脸
我弯过许多回腰
但还从没低过头
嗨，嗨，所以我想我过得不错

烦恼，啊，烦恼
烦恼在我心头
烦恼，啊，烦恼
烦恼在我心头
但世上的烦恼，主啊
比我的大得多

Hey, hey, so I guess I'm doin' fine

And I never had no armies
To jump at my command
No, I ain't got no armies
To jump at my command
But I don't need no armies
I got me one good friend
Hey, hey, so I guess I'm doin' fine

I been kicked and whipped and trampled on
I been shot at just like you
I been kicked and whipped and trampled on
I been shot at just like you.
But as long as the world keeps a- turnin'
I just keep a- turnin' too
Hey, hey, so I guess I'm doin' fine

Well, my road might be rocky
The stones might cut my face
My road it might be rocky
The stones might cut my face
But as some folks ain't got no road at all
They gotta stand in the same old place
Hey, hey, so I guess I'm doin' fine

嗨，嗨，所以我想我过得不错

我从来没有军队
立即执行我的命令
是的，我从来没有军队
立即执行我的命令
而我不需要军队
我有一个好朋友
嗨，嗨，所以我想我过得不错

我被踢过抽过践踏过
曾经中过枪，就跟你一样
我被踢过抽过践踏过
曾经中过枪，就跟你一样
但只要世界保持转动
我也就会保持转动
嗨，嗨，所以我想我过得不错

嗯，我的路可能磕磕绊绊
石头可能会划伤我的脸
我的路可能磕磕绊绊
石头可能会划伤我的脸
但有些人根本没路
他们必须站在原点
嗨，嗨，所以我想我过得不错

ANOTHER SIDE OF BOB DYLAN
鲍勃·迪伦的另一面

Some
other kinds
of songs...

Poems by Bob Dylan

---

baby black's
been had
aint bad
smokestacked
chicken shacked
dressed in black
silver monkey
on her back
mammy ma
juiced pa
janitored
between the
brothers tax
rat-faced
gravestoned
ditch dug
firescaped an substroked
choked
baby black
hits back
robs, pawns
lives by the
sits an waits
digs the her
eyes meet
picket line
across the
head rings
of bed springs
freedom
you ask
sho'el t
the w
for a dollar an
baby black in
dressed in
gunny sack
about t crack
been gone
carry on
i'm givin up
myself t pawn

for françoise hardy
at the seine's edge
a giant shadow
of notre d
sorbonne
whirl by an
swirlin litch
the breeze
far from the
of erhard
piles of lovers
fishing
kissing
lay themselves on their books, boats,
old men
clothed in curly mustaches
float on the benches
blankets of tourists
in bright red nylon shirts
with straw hats of ambassadors
(cannot hear nixon's
dawn bark now)
will sail away
as the sun goes down
the doors of the river are open
i must remember that

"what d you mean?"
"i mean i lose all the time"
his jaw tightened an he took
a deep breath
"hummin, now i gotta beat you"

straight away an into the ring
juno takes twenty pills an
paints all day. life he says
is a head kinda thing. outside
of chicago, private coma down
junkie nurse home heals countless
common housewives strung out
fully on drugstore dope. legally
sold t help clean the kitchen.
lenny bruce shows his seventh
avenue hand made movies, while a
bunch of women sneak little white
tablets into shoes, stockings, hats
an other hidin places, newspapers
tell neither. irma goes t israel
an writes me that there, they
hate nazis much more n we over here
do. nice an dies yes, an west
pruned out gestapo minds run
the penitentiary. in east berlin
renata tells me that i must wear
t get in t this certain place
one must have some sign says he wo
t be shot. everyone some time too
gestapo minds run the ford
should keep his mouth shut
lya head on the grass an my hair
up an hands feather t another
little boy who immediately falls
down. "it's my turn t be the good
guy... take that, redskin" bang bang
henry miller stands on other side
of ping pong table an keeps
yellin at me "did you ask
that fellow if he wants
anyone getttin an
enemies dont even put me down
n such a mysterious way
microphone an tape recorder
think your question
it rattles off james an numbers
you dont
general your
fortune
tell your wishes flowing
fingers pointed
i'm monstrously against the
unamerican activities commi tee
an alse the cia an i beg her please
not t ask me why for it would take
too long t tell she asks me about
humanity an i say i'm not sure
what that word means. she wants me
t say what she wants me t say. she
wants not t say what she
can understand. a loose tempered fat
man in borrowed stomach slams wife
in the face an rushes off t civil
rights meeting. while some strange
girl chases me up smoky mountain
tryin t find out what sign i am.
i take allen ginsberg t meet fantastic

between pillars of chips
springs on their
thumps thumps
strikes
is on the prowl
you'll only lose
shouldnt stay.
jack o' diamonds
is a hard t play

jack o' diamonds
wrecked my hand
left me here t stand
little tin men play
their drums now
upside my head
in the midst of cheers
flowers
four queens
with pawed out hearts
make make believe
they're stull good
but i should drop

should apolo
ho hun
wierd table taken
young babies horseback ride
their fathers' necks
two dudes in hopped up ford
for the tenth time
have rolled thru town
its your turn baby t
der
stayed too long
chinese gong
down the way
says jack o' diamonds
(a high card)
jack o' diamonds
(but ain't high enough)

jack o' diamonds
is a hard card t play

jack o' diamonds used t laugh
now wants t collect from me
need t be ashamed of me
now wants t walk long side of
jack o' diamonds
one armed prince
aras but a single glove.
as he shoves
never loves
the moon's too bright
as he's fixed mirrors
round the room at nite
it's hard t think
there's probably somethin
in my drink
should pour it out
inside the sink
would throw it in his face
but it'd do no good
give no gain
just leave a stain
jack o' diamonds
an all his crap
needs some acid
in his lap
what hour now
it feels late somehow
my hounddog bays
need more ashtrays
i cant even remember
the early days
please dont stay
gather your bells an go
jack o' diamonds
(can open for riches)
jack o' diamonds

(handwritten overlay:)

It aint me babe it aint me you're looking for

Oh you say that you are looking
for someone who is strong
t ~~protect~~ protect you ~~for from~~ from all
sadness
an defend you right or wrong
but

Oh you say
oh you say that
~~~~ you are looking
for ~~a~~ heart t be so true
someone you can count on hot t leave
an t love nothing else but you
youll eyes
your words
your whispering
but I'm afraid I aint t be going
they run
tell your fortune
tell your wishes flowing
tell the water there is flowing

1964 年 8 月 8 日，哥伦比亚唱片公司发行了迪伦的第 4 张录音室专辑，《鲍勃·迪伦的另一面》。

是年 2 月，迪伦与几个朋友乘坐着旅行车，进行了为期 3 周的横穿美国之旅，仿佛杰克·凯鲁亚克小说《在路上》的情景。《自由的钟声》都是旅途中的产物。

车过科罗拉多，车载收音机播放着排行榜歌曲，十中有八是披头士乐队的歌。当听到《我想握着你的手》（"I Want to Hold Your Hand"）时，迪伦"差点从车上跳下来"。他对伙伴们说："你们听到了吗？这太棒了！天啊……"此前迪伦听过披头士乐队的歌，称其为"泡泡糖"，但这次感觉不同："他们正在做一些没人做过的事。他们的和弦令人发指，简直是令人发指，但他们的和声让这一切变得合理……"[1] 3 月份一回到纽约，迪伦就租了一把电吉他。

也是回到纽约后，迪伦与苏西发生争执。这次争吵彻底结束了二人的关系。

---

[1] Hajdu, David (2001). *Positively 4th Street : the lives and times of Joan Baez, Bob Dylan, Mimi Baez Fariña, and Richard Fariña*. London: Bloomsbury. p. 197.

5 月，迪伦前往英国演出，在欧洲游历了一番，结识了妮可（Nico）并结伴同游。在瑞典小村庄沃立亚歌美尼，迪伦完成了专辑中的大部分歌曲。

录音只花了一个晚上，6 月 9 日晚 7 点至次日凌晨 1 点半。进棚之前，制作人汤姆·威尔逊"对当晚要录的歌一无所知"，他所要做的就是帮迪伦排除一切技术障碍。6 个半小时，15 首迪伦的原创作品被录下，其中《丹尼丝》《妈妈，你一直在我心上》等被弃用。

《鲍勃·迪伦的另一面》中"没有一首批判歌曲"，不再做广泛的社会观察，偏出《时代正在改变》专辑中的社会意识。这一变化引起了民谣界的尖锐批评。

专辑中大部分都是情歌。情歌中的大部分，似乎都是分手歌，表达不得已的告别之意。很久以后人们意识到，这是迪伦式的情歌，带着分道扬镳的姿态。随着现代化的动荡在随后半个世纪里不断发生，我们发现该专辑中的歌曲也是时代歌曲。值得注意的是，在男女关系上，迪伦一方面对对方满含批评和讥讽，另一方面也不乏同情心和幽默。

这些歌曲从外界转向内心，从社会转向个人，是内在导向、内在探索、充满自我意识的。面对外界的批评，迪伦声称创作这些歌曲"只是因为我自己想要并且需要写"。他对记者纳特·亨托夫（Nat Hentoff）说："我不想再为了别人写歌，你知道，就像一个代言人。我想写我内心的东西，想找回 10 岁时的那种写作——所有东西都是自然流露的。我向往的，是像走路或说话一样自然而然的写作。"

《自由的钟声》《昨日书》是专辑中的异类。与《西班牙哈莱姆事件》类似，迪伦开始使用不常见的词语组合，歌词中充满了奇怪的复合意象，以唤起神秘感受，体现了法国象征主义进一步的影响。在 1964 年 2 月，迪伦曾告诉朋友们："兰波就是这样。这就是有意义的东西。这就是我要的写作。"兰波曾在一封信中写道："诗人通过长期的、庞大的和有理性的感官混乱使自己成为一位先知……他进入未知，即使疯狂地，最终失去了对他的幻象的理解，至少他已经看到了它们。"

《自由的钟声》和《昨日书》不只受到兰波的影响，更是迪伦个人风格的表达。《自由的钟声》以毫不掩饰的末日想象，展示了迪伦对自然伟力的神秘主义理解，其中，人世间所有的畸零人、被污辱和被损害者，都以神秘主义的方式得到了救赎并被拥抱。这首歌在宽广和雄浑的程度上达到了歌史上的极致，代表了迪伦在歌曲形式上的飞跃，迸发出更强烈、更广大、更复杂、更磅礴的诗意。《昨日书》在思想上似乎是反向的，通过反思过去，迪伦否定和放弃了以前过于严肃的救世主题。

《我将会自由第 10 号》与稍后创作的《汽车惊魂噩梦》，被有些评论称为"超现实主义的谈话布鲁斯"，它们以搞笑和反讽的叙事，反映了 20 世纪 60 年代反文化的兴起以及主流社会对此的刻板反应。

整张专辑展示了一个转变中的、全新的迪伦，有评论称之为"一张没有电吉他的摇滚专辑，建立起一种突破了吃苦耐劳、直言不讳模式的民谣歌曲原型"。

ALL I REALLY WANT TO DO

I ain't lookin' to compete with you
Beat or cheat or mistreat you
Simplify you, classify you
Deny, defy or crucify you
All I really want to do
Is, baby, be friends with you

No, and I ain't lookin' to fight with you
Frighten you or tighten you
Drag you down or drain you down
Chain you down or bring you down
All I really want to do
Is, baby, be friends with you

I ain't lookin' to block you up
Shock or knock or lock you up
Analyze you, categorize you
Finalize you or advertise you
All I really want to do
Is, baby, be friends with you

I don't want to straight-face you

我真正想做的事

我并不希望和你争
击败你、愚弄你或者欺负你
把你简化，将你分类
否定、蔑视或者教训你
我真正想做的事
就是，宝贝，与你做朋友

是的，我也不希望与你斗
让你恐惧或让你紧张
拖累你或者耗干你
捆住你或者搞倒你
我真正想做的事
就是，宝贝，与你做朋友

我并不希望给你限制
震惊、倾倒或者锁住你
将你解析，把你归档
给你定性或为你宣传
我真正想做的事
就是，宝贝，与你做朋友

我不想对你绷着脸

Race or chase you, track or trace you

Or disgrace you or displace you

Or define you or confine you

All I really want to do

Is, baby, be friends with you

I don't want to meet your kin

Make you spin or do you in

Or select you or dissect you

Or inspect you or reject you

All I really want to do

Is, baby, be friends with you

I don't want to fake you out

Take or shake or forsake you out

I ain't lookin' for you to feel like me

See like me or be like me

All I really want to do

Is, baby, be friends with you

跟你比赛或追逐，对你跟踪或尾随
羞辱你或取代你
定义你或限制你
我真正想做的事
就是，宝贝，与你做朋友

我不想见你亲戚
让你眩晕或让你疲惫
选取你或分析你
审查你或拒绝你
我真正想做的事
就是，宝贝，与你做朋友

我不想哄骗你
带你出去，或耍一耍，或把你抛弃
我不希望你跟我同样感受
像我一样理解或变得就像我
我真正想做的事
就是，宝贝，与你做朋友

BLACK CROW BLUES

I woke in the mornin', wand'rin'
Wasted and worn out
I woke in the mornin', wand'rin'
Wasted and worn out
Wishin' my long-lost lover
Will walk to me, talk to me
Tell me what it's all about

I was standin' at the side road
Listenin' to the billboard knock
Standin' at the side road
Listenin' to the billboard knock
Well, my wrist was empty
But my nerves were kickin'
Tickin' like a clock

If I got anything you need, babe
Let me tell you in front
If I got anything you need, babe
Let me tell you in front
You can come to me sometime
Night time, day time

黑乌鸦蓝调

我早上醒来，四处游荡
无聊却又疲惫
我早上醒来，四处游荡
无聊却又疲惫
多想我久别的爱人
会走过来，跟我说说话
告诉我这都是怎么回事

我站在侧路上
听广告牌砰砰响
站在侧路上
听广告牌砰砰响
哦，我的手腕空空
但神经在跳动
就像时钟嘀嗒作响

如果我有你需要的，宝贝
让我话说在前头
如果我有你需要的，宝贝
让我话说在前头
你可以找时间来我这儿
夜晚的时候，白天的时候

Any time you want

Sometimes I'm thinkin' I'm
Too high to fall
Sometimes I'm thinkin' I'm
Too high to fall
Other times I'm thinkin' I'm
So low I don't know
If I can come up at all

Black crows in the meadow
Across a broad highway
Black crows in the meadow
Across a broad highway
Though it's funny, honey
I just don't feel much like a
Scarecrow today

任何你想来的时候

有时我想象我
太高而无法下落
有时我想象我
太高而无法下落
又有时我想象我
那么低，我不知道我
还能不能上来

草地上的黑乌鸦
穿过宽阔的公路
草地上的黑乌鸦
穿过宽阔的公路
虽然这很好笑，亲爱的
只是我觉得今天我不太像是
一个稻草人

SPANISH HARLEM INCIDENT

Gypsy gal, the hands of Harlem
Cannot hold you to its heat
Your temperature's too hot for taming
Your flaming feet burn up the street
I am homeless, come and take me
Into reach of your rattling drums
Let me know, babe, about my fortune
Down along my restless palms

Gypsy gal, you got me swallowed
I have fallen far beneath
Your pearly eyes, so fast an' slashing
An' your flashing diamond teeth
The night is pitch black, come an' make my
Pale face fit into place, ah, please!
Let me know, babe, I'm nearly drowning
If it's you my lifelines trace

I been wond'rin' all about me

西班牙哈莱姆事件 [1]

吉卜赛姑娘，哈莱姆的双手
无法控制你在它的热度
你温度太高，无法驯服
街道焚毁于你燃烧的双足
我已无家可归，来牵着我啊
迎接进入你咚咚响的鼓
让我明白那命数，宝贝
沿着我掌心的不安纹路

吉卜赛姑娘，你吞下了我
我已深深地陷落
你珍珠的明眸，那么凌厉
还有你钻石般闪耀的皓齿
夜晚如黑沥青，来吧
让我苍白的脸融入，啊，求你！
请让我明白宝贝，我就快淹死了
而我的救生索追随的，是不是你

我惊异着身上的一切

---

[1] 西班牙哈莱姆，纽约曼哈顿区的一部分，第一次世界大战后波多黎
各移民大量涌入。本篇由杨盈盈校译。

Ever since I seen you there

On the cliffs of your wildcat charms I'm riding

I know I'm 'round you but I don't know where

You have slayed me, you have made me

I got to laugh halfways off my heels

I got to know, babe, will you surround me?

So I can tell if I'm really real

自从遇见你
我就骑在你野猫般魅力的悬崖上
知道我就在你身边，却不明白身在何处
你把我宰了，你把我造了
我笑得中途跑掉了鞋子
我必须知道宝贝，你会环绕着我吗？
这样我才能明辨我是否真的

CHIMES OF FREEDOM

Far between sundown's finish an' midnight's broken toll
We ducked inside the doorway, thunder crashing
As majestic bells of bolts struck shadows in the sounds
Seeming to be the chimes of freedom flashing
Flashing for the warriors whose strength is not to fight
Flashing for the refugees on the unarmed road of flight
An' for each an' ev'ry underdog soldier in the night
An' we gazed upon the chimes of freedom flashing

In the city's melted furnace, unexpectedly we watched
With faces hidden while the walls were tightening
As the echo of the wedding bells before the blowin' rain
Dissolved into the bells of the lightning
Tolling for the rebel, tolling for the rake
Tolling for the luckless, the abandoned an' forsaked
Tolling for the outcast, burnin' constantly at stake
An' we gazed upon the chimes of freedom flashing

Through the mad mystic hammering of the wild ripping hail
The sky cracked its poems in naked wonder

自由的钟声 [1]

太阳西沉，离午夜破空的钟鸣尚远
我们一头扎进门廊，雷声隆隆
闪电威严的钟，撞击巨响中的阴影
好像自由的钟声在闪亮
为力量不用于战斗的武士闪亮
为逃亡路上手无寸铁的难民闪亮
为黑夜中每一位落败的士兵闪亮
我们注视着自由的钟声在闪亮

这城市的熔炉，四壁收紧
此时我们藏起自己的脸，意外地观看着
婚礼的钟声回响在风雨之前
融入那闪电的钟
鸣响，为叛逆者；鸣响，为浪荡子
鸣响，为倒霉的、被放弃的、被抛舍的人
鸣响，为被驱逐者，他们在生死线上久久燃烧
我们注视着自由的钟声在闪亮

穿过野蛮肆虐的冰雹那疯狂神秘的锤击
天空以它一览无遗的奇迹爆裂出诗篇片片

---

[1]　本篇由郝佳校译。

That the clinging of the church bells blew far into the breeze

Leaving only bells of lightning and its thunder

Striking for the gentle, striking for the kind

Striking for the guardians and protectors of the mind

An' the unpawned painter behind beyond his rightful time

An' we gazed upon the chimes of freedom flashing

Through the wild cathedral evening the rain unraveled tales

For the disrobed faceless forms of no position

Tolling for the tongues with no place to bring their thoughts

All down in taken-for-granted situations

Tolling for the deaf an' blind, tolling for the mute

Tolling for the mistreated, mateless mother, the mistitled
   prostitute

For the misdemeanor outlaw, chased an' cheated by pursuit

An' we gazed upon the chimes of freedom flashing

Even though a cloud's white curtain in a far-off corner flashed

An' the hypnotic splattered mist was slowly lifting

Electric light still struck like arrows, fired but for the ones

Condemned to drift or else be kept from drifting

Tolling for the searching ones, on their speechless, seeking trail

For the lonesome-hearted lovers with too personal a tale

An' for each unharmful, gentle soul misplaced inside a jail

An' we gazed upon the chimes of freedom flashing

教堂钟声的余响远远地飘进微风之中
只留下闪电和雷鸣的钟
为温良的人而鸣，为友善的人而鸣
为心灵的卫士和监护人而鸣
为落后或超前于他的时代的背运画家而鸣
我们注视着自由的钟声在闪亮

穿过那疯狂的教堂之夜，那一场雨
为被剥光的无名的位卑的小人物，解开了一个个传说
鸣响，为无处说出思想的舌头
它们落入了理所当然的情境
鸣响，为聋人、盲人和哑巴
鸣响，为被虐待者、单身母亲和辱称的
　　妓女
为因品行不端而定罪的人，他们被通缉被欺骗被穷追不舍
我们注视着自由的钟声在闪亮

尽管一片云的白帘仍在遥远的角落频闪
而催人入眠的断续的雾正慢慢消散
电光依然闪耀，就像羽箭离弦
只为那些被宣判去流亡的和不准流亡的
鸣响，为上下求索的人，他们走在无言的、寻求的路上
为内心孤独的情侣，他们有着过于隐秘的故事
为冤狱的从未伤害别人的温良灵魂
我们注视着自由的钟声在闪亮

Starry-eyed an' laughing as I recall when we were caught

Trapped by no track of hours for they hanged suspended

As we listened one last time an' we watched with one last look

Spellbound an' swallowed 'til the tolling ended

Tolling for the aching ones whose wounds cannot be nursed

For the countless confused, accused, misused, strung-out ones
  an' worse

An' for every hung-up person in the whole wide universe

An' we gazed upon the chimes of freedom flashing

我眼放幻想，放声大笑，当回想起我们被迷醉的一刻
时间不再受限因为它被暂时挂起
我们最后一次去倾听，用最后一眼去注视
被咒语定住、被强力俘虏，直至那钟声消逝
那钟声为痛楚的人鸣响，他们的伤口无从疗治
为数不尽的困惑者、被告、毒虫、瘾君子以及
    更糟的
为广大宇宙中每一个想不通的人鸣响
我们注视着自由的钟声在闪亮

I SHALL BE FREE NO. 10

I'm just average, common too
I'm just like him, the same as you
I'm everybody's brother and son
I ain't different from anyone
It ain't no use a-talking to me
It's just the same as talking to you

I was shadow-boxing earlier in the day
I figured I was ready for Cassius Clay
I said "Fee, fie, fo, fum, Cassius Clay, here I come
26, 27, 28, 29, I'm gonna make your face look just like mine
Five, four, three, two, one, Cassius Clay you'd better run
99, 100, 101, 102, your ma won't even recognize you
14, 15, 16, 17, 18, 19, gonna knock him clean right out of his
    spleen"

Well, I don't know, but I've been told
The streets in heaven are lined with gold
I ask you how things could get much worse
If the Russians happen to get up there first

我很平凡，也很普通
就像是他，和你一样
我是大家的兄弟和儿子
跟任何人都并无不同
跟我说话没什么用
就像跟你说话一样

我白天一大早就在打空拳
假想在迎战卡修斯·克莱[1]
我说："嘿、哈、呼、嗨，卡修斯·克莱，我来啦
26、27、28、29，我要让你的脸看上去像我的
五、四、三、二、一，卡修斯·克莱你最好快跑
99、100、101、102，你妈都认不出你来啦
14、15、16、17、18、19，要把他打得彻底
　　没脾气"

哦，我不知道，但有人告诉我
天堂的街道铺满了金子
我问你事情怎么会糟成这样
万一俄国人碰巧先到了那儿

---

[1] 卡修斯·克莱，拳王阿里的原名。

Wowee! pretty scary!

Now, I'm liberal, but to a degree
I want ev'rybody to be free
But if you think that I'll let Barry Goldwater
Move in next door and marry my daughter
You must think I'm crazy!
I wouldn't let him do it for all the farms in Cuba

Well, I set my monkey on the log
And ordered him to do the Dog
He wagged his tail and shook his head
And he went and did the Cat instead
He's a weird monkey, very funky

I sat with my high-heeled sneakers on
Waiting to play tennis in the noonday sun
I had my white shorts rolled up past my waist
And my wig-hat was falling in my face
But they wouldn't let me on the tennis court

I got a woman, she's so mean
She sticks my boots in the washing machine
Sticks me with buckshot when I'm nude

啊哈！非常可怕！

瞧，我是自由党，不过只到某个程度
我希望人人自由
但如果你觉得我会让巴里·戈德华特[1]
住到隔壁，并且娶我女儿
你一定认为我疯了！
我不会让他得逞，为了古巴所有的农场

哦，我把我的猴子放在原木上
命令它模仿狗
它摇摇尾巴，晃晃脑袋
反而做出了猫的样子
它是只怪猴子，非常奇怪

我穿高跟运动鞋坐着
等着在正午阳光里打网球
我把白短裤卷过了腰
而我的假发帽遮盖到脸上
可他们不让我上场

我有个女人，她真是卑鄙
把我的靴子丢进洗衣机
在我脱光时拿铅弹硌我

---

[1] 巴里·戈德华特，美国政客，共和党人，保守派。

Puts bubblegum in my food

She's funny, wants my money, calls me "honey"

Now I got a friend who spends his life

Stabbing my picture with a bowie knife

Dreams of strangling me with a scarf

When my name comes up he pretends to barf

I've got a million friends!

Now they asked me to read a poem

At the sorority sisters' home

I got knocked down and my head was swimmin'

I wound up with the Dean of Women

Yippee! I'm a poet, and I know it

Hope I don't blow it

I'm gonna grow my hair down to my feet so strange

So I look like a walking mountain range

And I'm gonna ride into Omaha on a horse

Out to the country club and the golf course

Carry *The New York Times*, shoot a few holes, blow their minds

Now you're probably wondering by now

Just what this song is all about

还把泡泡糖放入我的饭食中
她很好笑，想要我的钱，叫我"亲爱的"

嗯，我有个朋友，花了一辈子
用猎刀戳我的照片
梦想着用围巾勒死我
一提我的名字他就装呕吐
我有一百万个朋友！

你看，他们要我在
姐妹联谊会之家读诗
我被擂倒了，一阵头晕目眩
最后被女教长弄得飘飘然
好啊！我是个诗人，这我知道
希望我不会搞砸

我要留长发留到脚跟，这么怪
所以看上去就像是一列行走的山脉
我还要打马驰入奥马哈 [1]
驰入乡村俱乐部和高尔夫球场
带着《纽约时报》，打进几洞，让他们震惊

嗯，可能你一直在想，迄今为止
这首歌究竟在唱什么

---

[1] 奥马哈，美国城市，在内布拉斯加州。

What's probably got you baffled more

Is what this thing here is for

It's nothing

It's something I learned over in England

可能更让你头疼的是

这东西有什么用

它什么都不是

这是我在英格兰学到的玩意儿

TO RAMONA

Ramona

Come closer

Shut softly your watery eyes

The pangs of your sadness

Shall pass as your senses will rise

The flowers of the city

Though breathlike

Get deathlike at times

And there's no use in tryin'

T' deal with the dyin'

Though I cannot explain that in lines

Your cracked country lips

I still wish to kiss

As to be under the strength of your skin

Your magnetic movements

Still capture the minutes I'm in

But it grieves my heart, love

To see you tryin' to be a part of

A world that just don't exist

致拉莫娜 [1]

拉莫娜

靠近来

轻轻闭上你的泪眼

就让那悲伤的痛楚

随着你清醒的意识过去

这城市中的花

虽似在呼吸

有时却也一片死寂

不要去对付死亡

这只会是徒劳

虽然我不能三言两语解释

你干裂的乡村的唇

我依然渴求一吻

就像置身于你肌肤的力量下

你充满磁力的一举一动

依然捕获我的每一分钟

可是爱人，看你在努力成为

一个并不存在的世界的一部分

我的心又在伤痛

---

[1]　本篇由杨盈盈校译。

It's all just a dream, babe

A vacuum, a scheme, babe

That sucks you into feelin' like this

I can see that your head

Has been twisted and fed

By worthless foam from the mouth

I can tell you are torn

Between stayin' and returnin'

On back to the South

You've been fooled into thinking

That the finishin' end is at hand

Yet there's no one to beat you

No one t' defeat you

'Cept the thoughts of yourself feeling bad

I've heard you say many times

That you're better 'n no one

And no one is better 'n you

If you really believe that

You know you got

Nothing to win and nothing to lose

From fixtures and forces and friends

Your sorrow does stem

That hype you and type you

Making you feel

这只是一个梦，宝贝
一个虚空，一场阴谋，宝贝
却将你吸入了这一种感觉

我能看见你
为那一文不值的口吐的白沫
扭过头去
我看得很清楚
你在留下来
还是返回南方之间撕扯
你受了愚弄
以为终点就在近前
然而没人要打败你
没人要征服你
你只是自己感到难过

我听你说过好多次
你并不比谁好
谁也不比你好
如果你真的相信这些
你就明白你无可获取
也无可失去
你的悲伤实在是源于
常客、强势人物和友人们
他们炒热你，将你归类
让你感到

That you must be exactly like them

I'd forever talk to you
But soon my words
They would turn into a meaningless ring
For deep in my heart
I know there is no help I can bring
Everything passes
Everything changes
Just do what you think you should do
And someday maybe
Who knows, baby
I'll come and be cryin' to you

你必须跟他们一样

我永远愿意与你说话
但很快我的言语
就会变成无意义的回响
因为在内心深处我知道
我什么也帮不了你
一切都在逝去
一切都在改变
尽管去做你认为该做的吧
说不定有一天
谁知道呢，宝贝
我会跑过来，对着你哭泣

MOTORPSYCHO NIGHTMARE

I pounded on a farmhouse
Lookin' for a place to stay
I was mighty, mighty tired
I had come a long, long way
I said, "Hey, hey, in there
Is there anybody home?"
I was standin' on the steps
Feelin' most alone
Well, out comes a farmer
He must have thought that I was nuts
He immediately looked at me
And stuck a gun into my guts

I fell down
To my bended knees
Saying, "I dig farmers
Don't shoot me, please!"
He cocked his rifle
And began to shout

汽车惊魂噩梦 [1]

我重重敲着农舍门
想找个地方住
我极其极其疲惫
走了很长很长的路
我说："嗨，嗨，里面
有人在家吗？"
我站在台阶上
感到非常孤独
好了，一个农夫出来了
一定以为我是疯子
他一看到我
立即拿枪顶住我的肚子

我跪下了
双膝屈地
说："我喜欢农夫
别开枪，求你！"
他扳上扳机
然后开始大喊

---

[1] 歌名及歌词涉及希区柯克执导的电影《惊魂记》（*Psycho*, 1960）。

"You're that travelin' salesman
That I have heard about"

I said, "No! No! No!
I'm a doctor and it's true
I'm a clean-cut kid
And I been to college, too"

Then in comes his daughter
Whose name was Rita
She looked like she stepped out of
La Dolce Vita
I immediately tried to cool it
With her dad
And told him what a
Nice, pretty farm he had
He said, "What do doctors
Know about farms, pray tell?"
I said, "I was born
At the bottom of a wishing well"

Well, by the dirt 'neath my nails

"你是那个旅行推销员 [1]
我听说过"

我说:"不! 不! 不!
我是个医生,真的
我是个清白人
而且我还上过大学"

然后他女儿来了
她名叫丽塔
看起来就像是
从《甜蜜的生活》[2] 走出来的
我立刻试着
让她爸爸冷静
并且告诉他,他有一个
多么好、多么美的农场
他说:"对于农场
医生们都知道什么,请讲?"
我说:"我出生在
一个许愿井的井底"

哦,凭我指甲里的泥

---

[1] 英语笑话常拿旅行推销员背着农夫与其女儿发生关系为笑谈。

[2] 《甜蜜的生活》,费里尼 1960 年执导的电影,出演女主角的安妮
塔·艾克伯格因此走红,成为性感女郎的代名词。

I guess he knew I wouldn't lie
"I guess you're tired"
He said, kinda sly
I said, "Yes, ten thousand miles
Today I drove"
He said, "I got a bed for you
Underneath the stove
Just one condition
And you go to sleep right now
That you don't touch my daughter
And in the morning, milk the cow"

I was sleepin' like a rat
When I heard something jerkin'
There stood Rita
Lookin' just like Tony Perkins
She said, "Would you like to take a shower?
I'll show you up to the door"
I said, "Oh, no! no!
I've been through this before"
I knew I had to split
But I didn't know how
When she said

我猜他知道了我不会撒谎

"我想你累了"

他有些会意地说

我说："确实，我今天开车

跑了一万英里"

他说："我给你弄张床

就在炉子下方

只有一个条件

你现在就去睡觉

别碰我女儿

到了早上，给奶牛挤奶"

我睡得像只老鼠

直到听到猛然有东西

丽塔站在那里

看起来就像托尼·珀金斯 [1]

她说："你要冲澡吗？

我带你到门口去"

我说："噢，不！不！

我已经去过了"

我知道我得赶紧走

但我不知道该怎么做

当她说

---

[1] 即安东尼·珀金斯，美国演员，在《惊魂记》中扮演具有双重人格的汽车旅馆老板，在浴室中杀死了卷款潜逃的女主角。

"Would you like to take that shower, now?"

Well, I couldn't leave
Unless the old man chased me out
'Cause I'd already promised
That I'd milk his cows
I had to say something
To strike him very weird
So I yelled out
"I like Fidel Castro and his beard"
Rita looked offended
But she got out of the way
As he came charging down the stairs
Sayin', "What's that I heard you say?"

I said, "I like Fidel Castro
I think you heard me right"
And ducked as he swung
At me with all his might
Rita mumbled something
'Bout her mother on the hill
As his fist hit the icebox
He said he's going to kill me
If I don't get out the door

"你要冲澡吗，现在？"

唉，我不能走
除非那老头儿赶我出去
因为我已经答应过
要给他的奶牛挤奶
我得说点什么
很怪异地顶撞他
于是我喊道
"我喜欢菲德尔·卡斯特罗 [1] 和他的胡子"
丽塔看起来受了冒犯
可她走开了
这时他冲下楼梯
说："我听到你说了什么？"

我说："我喜欢菲德尔·卡斯特罗
我想你没听错"
然后低了头，当他用尽力气
向我挥舞拳头
丽塔喃喃自语
说着她山上的母亲
这时他用拳猛击冰箱
说要杀了我
如果我不在两秒钟内

---

[1] 菲德尔·卡斯特罗，古巴领导人，与美国为敌。

In two seconds flat
"You unpatriotic
Rotten doctor Commie rat"

Well, he threw a *Reader's Digest*
At my head and I did run
I did a somersault
As I seen him get his gun
And crashed through the window
At a hundred miles an hour
And landed fully blast
In his garden flowers
Rita said, "Come back!"
As he started to load
The sun was comin' up
And I was runnin' down the road

Well, I don't figure I'll be back
There for a spell
Even though Rita moved away
And got a job in a motel
He still waits for me
Constant, on the sly
He wants to turn me in
To the F.B.I.
Me, I romp and stomp

滚出门
"你这不爱国的
烂医生,一介鼠辈"

哦,他将一本《读者文摘》
砸我头上,我就跑了
我翻了个跟头
当我看见他拿枪
我撞开了窗子
以时速一百英里
轰然坠地
就在他花园的花丛里
丽塔说:"回来!"
这时他开始上弹药
太阳出来了
我顺着大路跑去

哦,我想我不会回去了
哪怕一小会儿
尽管丽塔搬走了
在汽车旅馆打份儿工
他还在等着我
始终如一,摸摸索索
要去告发我
到联邦调查局
我呢,我嬉笑、跺脚

Thankful as I romp

Without freedom of speech

I might be in the swamp

嬉笑时庆幸

若没有言论自由

可能我已身陷泥沼 [1]

---

[1] 《惊魂记》中，凶手杀害女主角后，弃尸泥沼。

MY BACK PAGES

Crimson flames tied through my ears
Rollin' high and mighty traps
Pounced with fire on flaming roads
Using ideas as my maps
"We'll meet on edges, soon," said I
Proud 'neath heated brow
Ah, but I was so much older then
I'm younger than that now

Half-wracked prejudice leaped forth
"Rip down all hate," I screamed
Lies that life is black and white
Spoke from my skull. I dreamed
Romantic facts of musketeers
Foundationed deep, somehow
Ah, but I was so much older then
I'm younger than that now

Girls' faces formed the forward path
From phony jealousy

昨日书

深红色火舌穿过我双耳
翻卷过高高的强力陷阱
被火红道路上的烈焰扑住
以意念作为我的导图
"很快，我们就会在边界重逢。"我说
眉宇间意气风发
啊，昔日我如此苍老
如今却风华正茂

残存的偏见跳了出来
"撕下所有仇恨。"我叫道
人生非黑即白的谎言
从我头颅深处冒出。我梦见
三个火枪手的浪漫纪事 [1]
不知为何，这样根深蒂固
啊，昔日我如此苍老
如今却风华正茂

女孩们的面孔铺就了前行道路
从虚假的嫉妒

---

[1] 语涉大仲马小说《三个火枪手》。

To memorizing politics

Of ancient history

Flung down by corpse evangelists

Unthought of, though, somehow

Ah, but I was so much older then

I'm younger than that now

A self-ordained professor's tongue

Too serious to fool

Spouted out that liberty

Is just equality in school

"Equality," I spoke the word

As if a wedding vow

Ah, but I was so much older then

I'm younger than that now

In a soldier's stance, I aimed my hand

At the mongrel dogs who teach

Fearing not that I'd become my enemy

In the instant that I preach

My pathway led by confusion boats

Mutiny from stern to bow

Ah, but I was so much older then

I'm younger than that now

Yes, my guard stood hard when abstract threats

到古代历史
记住的政治
都被死尸布道者抛下
然而不知为何，我从不在意
啊，昔日我如此苍老
如今却风华正茂

自命的教授大放厥词
一本正经得不容开玩笑
口若悬河说着那自由
只不过是校园里的平等
"平等。"我说出这个词
就像说出结婚誓言
啊，昔日我如此苍老
如今却风华正茂

以一个战士的姿态，我将手
指向那帮教导人的杂种
无惧于在我宣讲的一刻
我会变成自己的敌人
我的道路为迷舟指引
从船尾到船头全部哗变
啊，昔日我如此苍老
如今却风华正茂

是的，我的卫士严阵以待，当观念的威胁

Too noble to neglect

Deceived me into thinking

I had something to protect

Good and bad, I define these terms

Quite clear, no doubt, somehow

Ah, but I was so much older then

I'm younger than that now

高尚得无法忽视
误导我去思考
以为我真有什么要去捍卫
善与恶，我定义这些词
不知为何极其清晰，毋庸置疑
啊，昔日我如此苍老
如今却风华正茂

I DON'T BELIEVE YOU
(SHE ACTS LIKE WE NEVER HAVE MET)

I can't understand
She let go of my hand
An' left me here facing the wall
I'd sure like t' know
Why she did go
But I can't get close t' her at all
Though we kissed through the wild blazing nighttime
She said she would never forget
But now mornin's clear
It's like I ain't here
She just acts like we never have met

It's all new t' me
Like some mystery
It could even be like a myth
Yet it's hard t' think on
That she's the same one
That last night I was with
From darkness, dreams're deserted

不相信你
（她表现得好像我们从不认识）[1]

我如何能理解

她竟放开我的手

丢下我，在这儿面对墙壁

我真想知道

她为什么要走

但我已完全不能再接近

虽然我们曾在狂野的燃情之夜亲吻

她说永远不会忘记

但此时晨光明澈

好像我并不在此处

她表现得好像我们从不认识

这于我是全新体验

就像一种谜

甚至像一个神话

但还是难以想象

她就是昨夜和我

在一起的同一人

自黑暗中，梦被遗弃

---

[1] 本篇由杨盈盈校译。

Am I still dreamin' yet?

I wish she'd unlock

Her voice once an' talk

'Stead of acting like we never have met

If she ain't feelin' well

Then why don't she tell

'Stead of turnin' her back t' my face?

Without any doubt

She seems too far out

For me t' return t' her chase

Though the night ran swirling an' whirling

I remember her whispering yet

But evidently she don't

An' evidently she won't

She just acts like we never have met

If I didn't have t' guess

I'd gladly confess

T' anything I might've tried

If I was with 'er too long

Or have done something wrong

I wish she'd tell me what it is, I'll run an' hide

Though her skirt it swayed as a guitar played

Her mouth was watery and wet

But now something has changed

而我还在做梦？
我希望她能来解答
用她的嗓音再一次，说说话
而不是表现得好像我们从不认识

假若她感觉不佳
那她为什么不明说
非要将后背对着我？
毫无疑问
她似乎已走远
我无法再让她回心转意
虽然那个夜晚地转天旋
我还记得她的耳语
但是她显然不这样
显然她也不会
她表现得好像我们从不认识

假若我不用猜测
那么我很乐意去忏悔
为我可能做过的一切
是否我跟她在一起太久
或者做错了什么
希望她明白告诉我，我会躲得远远的
虽然她裙裾摇曳如吉他弹拨
她的唇湿润又多汁
但是现在情况变了

For she ain't the same

She just acts like we never have met

I'm leavin' today

I'll be on my way

Of this I can't say very much

But if you want me to

I can be just like you

An' pretend that we never have touched

An' if anybody asks me

"Is it easy to forget?"

I'll say, "It's easily done

You just pick anyone

An' pretend that you never have met!"

她已不似从前
她表现得好像我们从不认识

今天我就动身离开
将走上我的路
对此我不能说太多
但如果你要我说
我会变得跟你一样
假装我们从未见过
而如果有人问
"遗忘是否容易？"
我会说："容易之极
你随便挑个人
然后假装你们从不认识！"

BALLAD IN PLAIN D

I once loved a girl, her skin it was bronze
With the innocence of a lamb, she was gentle like a fawn
I courted her proudly but now she is gone
Gone as the season she's taken

Through young summer's breeze, I stole her away
From her mother and sister, though close did they stay
Each one of them suffering from the failures of their day
With strings of guilt they tried hard to guide us

Of the two sisters, I loved the young
With sensitive instincts, she was the creative one
The constant scapegoat, she was easily undone
By the jealousy of others around her

For her parasite sister, I had no respect
Bound by her boredom, her pride to protect
Countless visions of the other she'd reflect
As a crutch for her scenes and her society

直白的 D 大调情歌 [1]

我爱过一个姑娘，她的皮肤是古铜色的
羔羊般纯洁，又如小鹿一样温柔
我曾骄傲地追求她，而今她走了
走了，就像她带走的季节

借着年轻夏日的微风，我偷走了她
从她母亲和她姐姐那里，虽然她们很亲密
她们俩都被当年的挫败折磨着
带着连串悔恨，极力要引导我们

在两姐妹中，我爱上了妹妹
她天生敏锐，富有创造力
一直都是替罪羊，很容易
被周围人的嫉妒给毁了

对她的寄生虫姐姐，我毫无敬意
受缚于她的无趣，她必须捍卫的自尊
她反射着另一个人的无数幻影
作为对她的圈子和她的社交的支撑

------

[1] 这首歌记述了 1964 年 3 月迪伦与苏西关系破裂当晚的情景。

Myself, for what I did, I cannot be excused
The changes I was going through can't even be used
For the lies that I told her in hopes not to lose
The could-be dream-lover of my lifetime

With unknown consciousness, I possessed in my grip
A magnificent mantelpiece, though its heart being chipped
Noticing not that I'd already slipped
To a sin of love's false security

From silhouetted anger to manufactured peace
Answers of emptiness, voice vacancies
Till the tombstones of damage read me no questions but, "Please
What's wrong and what's exactly the matter?"

And so it did happen like it could have been foreseen
The timeless explosion of fantasy's dream
At the peak of the night, the king and the queen
Tumbled all down into pieces

"The tragic figure!" her sister did shout
"Leave her alone, God damn you, get out!"
And I in my armor, turning about
And nailing her to the ruins of her pettiness

Beneath a bare lightbulb the plaster did pound

我自己，对于我的所为，无可辩解
我正经历的改变甚至无法
编成谎话告诉她，以希望着不要失去
这可能是我一生的梦中爱侣

带着不自知的意识，我紧紧守护着
一座华丽的壁炉台，尽管它的中心已破碎
而没有留意到，我已经滑向了
爱的虚假担保之罪

从显形的愤怒到人造的和平
空洞的回答，沉默无声
直到损毁的墓碑再读不出我的问题，只有："求你了
怎么了，到底怎么回事？"

所以事情确实发生了，就像事先可以预见的
幻想之梦无休无止地爆炸
在夜晚之巅，国王和王后跌了下来
摔成了碎片

"可悲的人！"她姐姐喊道
"别碰她，该死的，滚出去！"
而我身披盔甲，回转身
把她钉在她小气的废墟上

在一只光秃秃的灯泡下面，石膏噼啪作响

Her sister and I in a screaming battleground
And she in between, the victim of sound
Soon shattered as a child 'neath her shadows

All is gone, all is gone, admit it, take flight
I gagged twice, doubled, tears blinding my sight
My mind it was mangled, I ran into the night
Leaving all of love's ashes behind me

The wind knocks my window, the room it is wet
The words to say I'm sorry, I haven't found yet
I think of her often and hope whoever she's met
Will be fully aware of how precious she is

Ah, my friends from the prison, they ask unto me
"How good, how good does it feel to be free?"
And I answer them most mysteriously
"Are birds free from the chains of the skyway?"

她姐姐和我在尖叫的战场上
而她夹在中间，噪声的受害者
很快万念俱灰，像一个孩子躲进她的影子里

都完了，都完了，承认吧，逃走吧
我哽咽两次，躬身，泪水遮住视线
我的意识模糊了，我跑进黑夜
将爱的所有灰烬抛在后面

风敲打着窗子，房间一片潮湿
说我很抱歉的措辞，我还没找到
我经常想起她，多希望她遇到的人
能完全意识到她是多么珍贵

啊，我狱中的朋友，他们问我
"多好啊，自由的感觉有多好呢？"
而我的回答神秘至极
"鸟儿能摆脱天上的路获得自由吗？"

IT AIN'T ME, BABE

Go 'way from my window
Leave at your own chosen speed
I'm not the one you want, babe
I'm not the one you need
You say you're lookin' for someone
Never weak but always strong
To protect you an' defend you
Whether you are right or wrong
Someone to open each and every door
But it ain't me, babe
No, no, no, it ain't me, babe
It ain't me you're lookin' for, babe

Go lightly from the ledge, babe
Go lightly on the ground
I'm not the one you want, babe
I will only let you down
You say you're lookin' for someone
Who will promise never to part
Someone to close his eyes for you
Someone to close his heart
Someone who will die for you an' more

这不是我，宝贝

离开我的窗子吧

紧走慢走随你的便

我不是你想要的人，宝贝

我不是你需要的人

你说你在找一个

永远坚强从不软弱

保护你并为你辩护的人

不管你是对是错

一个会把所有门都为你打开的人

但这不是我，宝贝

不不不，这不是我，宝贝

我不是你要找的人，宝贝

轻轻离开窗台吧，宝贝

轻轻走到地上

我不是你想要的人，宝贝

我只会让你失望

你说你在找一个

发誓永不分开的人

一个为你闭上眼睛的人

一个关上了心扉的人

一个不只会为你死的人

But it ain't me, babe
No, no, no, it ain't me, babe
It ain't me you're lookin' for, babe

Go melt back into the night, babe
Everything inside is made of stone
There's nothing in here moving
An' anyway I'm not alone
You say you're looking for someone
Who'll pick you up each time you fall
To gather flowers constantly
An' to come each time you call
A lover for your life an' nothing more
But it ain't me, babe
No, no, no, it ain't me, babe
It ain't me you're lookin' for, babe

但这不是我，宝贝

不不不，这不是我，宝贝

我不是你要找的人，宝贝

去融回到黑夜里吧，宝贝

其中万物都是石头做成

一切皆永恒不动

可不管怎样我都并非独自一人

你说你在找一个

每次跌倒都会扶起你的人

一直不停采花

每次招之即来

是你一生专属的爱人

但这可不是我，宝贝

不不不，这不是我，宝贝

我不是你要找的人，宝贝

DENISE

Denise, Denise
Gal, what's on your mind?
Denise, Denise
Gal, what's on your mind?
You got your eyes closed
Heaven knows that you ain't blind

Well, I can see you smiling
But oh your mouth is inside out
I can see you smiling
But you're smiling inside out
Well, I know you're laughin'
But what are you laughin' about

Well, if you're tryin' to throw me
Babe, I've already been tossed
If you're tryin' to throw me
Babe, I've already been tossed
Babe, you're tryin' to lose me
Babe, I'm already lost

Well, what are you doing

丹尼丝

丹尼丝，丹尼丝
姑娘，你在想什么呢？
丹尼丝，丹尼丝
姑娘，你在想什么呢？
你闭上了眼睛
天知道你不是盲人

好吧，我能看见你笑
不过啊，你的嘴都笑翻了
我能看见你笑
不过你都笑翻了
好吧，我知道你在大笑
但你笑什么呢

好吧，如果你想抛弃我
宝贝，我已经被甩掉了
如果你想抛弃我
宝贝，我已经被甩掉了
宝贝，你是想失去我
宝贝，我已经迷失掉了

那么，你在做什么

Are you flying or have you flipped?

Oh, what are you doing

Are you flying or have you flipped?

Well, you call my name

And then say your tongue just slipped

Denise, Denise

You're concealed here on the shelf

Denise, Denise

You're concealed here on the shelf

I'm looking deep in your eyes, babe

And all I can see is myself

你是在飞还是疯了？
哦，你在做什么
你是在飞还是疯了？
好吧，你在叫我的名字
然后说，你的舌头打滑了

丹尼丝，丹尼丝
你藏在这架子上
丹尼丝，丹尼丝
你藏在这架子上
我深望着你的眼，宝贝
我能看见的只是我自己

IF YOU GOTTA GO, GO NOW
(OR ELSE YOU GOT TO STAY ALL NIGHT)

Listen to me, baby

There's something you must see

I want to be with you, gal

If you want to be with me

But if you got to go

It's all right

But if you got to go, go now

Or else you gotta stay all night

It ain't that I'm questionin' you

To take part in any quiz

It's just that I ain't got no watch

An' you keep askin' me what time it is

But if you got to go

It's all right

But if you got to go, go now

Or else you gotta stay all night

I am just a poor boy, baby

如果你要走，现在就走
（不然就得留下过夜）

听我说，宝贝
有件事你一定得清楚
我想和你在一起，姑娘
如果你想和我在一起

但如果你要走
也没什么
但如果你要走，现在就走
不然就得留下过夜

我现在这样问你
并非要做测试
只是我没有手表
而你一直问我几点了

但如果你要走
也没什么
但如果你要走，现在就走
不然就得留下过夜

我只是个穷孩子，宝贝

Lookin' to connect

But I certainly don't want you thinkin'

That I ain't got any respect

But if you got to go

It's all right

But if you got to go, go now

Or else you gotta stay all night

You know I'd have nightmares

And a guilty conscience, too

If I kept you from anything

That you really wanted to do

But if you got to go

It's all right

But if you got to go, go now

Or else you gotta stay all night

It ain't that I'm wantin'

Anything you never gave before

It's just that I'll be sleepin' soon

It'll be too dark for you to find the door

But if you got to go

It's all right

指望着与人交朋友
但我当然不想让你觉得
我不需要得到尊重

但如果你要走
也没什么
但如果你要走，现在就走
不然就得留下过夜

你知道我会做噩梦
还有一种负罪心理
生怕妨碍了你
做你真正想做的事

但如果你要走
也没什么
但如果你要走，现在就走
不然就得留下过夜

我这并不是要得到
你以前没给过的东西
只是我就要睡了
天太黑了，你找不到门出去

但如果你要走
也没什么

But if you got to go, go now

Or else you gotta stay all night

但如果你要走，现在就走

不然就得留下过夜

MAMA, YOU BEEN ON MY MIND

Perhaps it's the color of the sun cut flat
An' cov'rin' the crossroads I'm standing at
Or maybe it's the weather or something like that
But mama, you been on my mind

I don't mean trouble, please don't put me down or get upset
I am not pleadin' or sayin', "I can't forget"
I do not walk the floor bowed down an' bent, but yet
Mama, you been on my mind

Even though my mind is hazy an' my thoughts they might be
   narrow
Where you been don't bother me nor bring me down in sorrow
It don't even matter to me where you're wakin' up tomorrow
But mama, you're just on my mind

I am not askin' you to say words like "yes" or "no"
Please understand me, I got no place for you t' go
I'm just breathin' to myself, pretendin' not that I don't know
Mama, you been on my mind

妈妈[1]，你一直在我心上

兴许是太阳的光彩被水平地切下
并覆盖了我伫立的这十字路口
或者也可能是天气或类似原因
但是妈妈，你一直在我心上

我不是有意找碴儿，请别奚落我也不要生气
我不是在恳求或说："我忘不掉"
我没有踱来踱去卑躬屈膝，可是
妈妈，你一直在我心上

纵使我脑子像团雾，想法也可能
　　偏狭
但你去了哪儿并不令我心烦或让我陷入悲伤
我甚至不在乎明天你在何处醒来
但是妈妈，你就是在我心上

我不是要你说"是"或"不是"之类
请理解我，我并没有地方非要你去
我只是在自己呼吸，假装我不知道
妈妈，你一直在我心上

―――――――

[1]　妈妈，俚语中"妈妈"是对情人的昵称。

When you wake up in the mornin', baby, look inside your
   mirror
You know I won't be next to you, you know I won't be near
I'd just be curious to know if you can see yourself as clear
As someone who has had you on his mind

当你早晨醒来，宝贝，看着
　镜子
你知道我不会在你身边，你知道我不会在近旁
我只是好奇你能否清晰地看到自己
就像把你放在心上的那个人一样

PLAYBOYS AND PLAYGIRLS

Oh, ye playboys and playgirls
Ain't a-gonna run my world
Ain't a-gonna run my world
Ain't a-gonna run my world
Ye playboys and playgirls
Ain't a-gonna run my world
Not now or no other time

You fallout shelter sellers
Can't get in my door
Can't get in my door
Can't get in my door
You fallout shelter sellers
Can't get in my door
Not now or no other time

Your Jim Crow ground
Can't turn me around
Can't turn me around
Can't turn me around
Your Jim Crow ground
Can't turn me around

花花公子和花花公主

啊，你们这些花花公子和花花公主

不会掌控我的世界

不会掌控我的世界

不会掌控我的世界

你们这些花花公子和花花公主

不会掌控我的世界

不管是现在还是他时

你们这些防核尘掩体的贩卖者

进不了我的门

进不了我的门

进不了我的门

你们这些防核尘掩体的贩卖者

进不了我的门

不管是现在还是他时

你们这吉姆·克劳之地

不可能让我转身

不可能让我转身

不可能让我转身

你们这些吉姆·克劳之地

不可能让我转身

Not now or no other time

The laughter in the lynch mob
Ain't a-gonna do no more
Ain't a-gonna do no more
Ain't a-gonna do no more
The laughter in the lynch mob
Ain't a-gonna do no more
Not now or no other time

You insane tongues of war talk
Ain't a-gonna guide my road
Ain't a-gonna guide my road
Ain't a-gonna guide my road
You insane tongues of war talk
Ain't a-gonna guide my road
Not now or no other time

You red baiters and race haters
Ain't a-gonna hang around here
Ain't a-gonna hang around here
Ain't a-gonna hang around here
You red baiters and race haters
Ain't a-gonna hang around here
Not now or no other time

不管是现在还是他时

动用私刑的暴民的笑
不会再有了
不会再有了
不会再有了
动用私刑的暴民的笑
不会再有了
不管是现在还是他时

你们这些大谈战争的发狂舌头
不会导引我的路
不会导引我的路
不会导引我的路
你们这些大谈战争的发狂舌头
不会导引我的路
不管是现在还是他时

你们这些麦卡锡主义者和种族仇恨分子
不会吊死在这附近
不会吊死在这附近
不会吊死在这附近
你们这些麦卡锡主义者和种族仇恨分子
不会吊死在这附近
不管是现在还是他时

Ye playboys and playgirls

Ain't a-gonna own my world

Ain't a-gonna own my world

Ain't a-gonna own my world

Ye playboys and playgirls

Ain't a-gonna own my world

Not now or no other time

你们这些花花公子和花花公主

不会拥有我的世界

不会拥有我的世界

不会拥有我的世界

你们这些花花公子和花花公主

不会拥有我的世界

不管是现在还是他时